Range of Light
The Sierra Nevada

Range of
THE SIERRA

PHIL SCHERMEISTER AND NOEL GROVE

NATIONAL GEOGRAPHIC

WASHINGTON, D.C.

Light

N E V A D A

CONTENTS

PAGE ONE: *The Tuolumne River flows beneath a pine branch in Stanislaus National Forest.*
PRECEDING PAGES: *Sunset bathes a distant ridge in gold on the north shore of Eagle Lake in Sequoia National Park.*
FACING PAGE: *A shaft of early sun spotlights steam rising off the West Fork of the Carson River in Toiyabe National Forest.*

Copyright notice and Library of Congress CIP data appear on page 200.

"MOST DIVINELY

BEAUTIFUL"

THE BIGGEST SNOWFALL IN YEARS COVERS BOTH THE MOUNTAINS AND the desert below in a coat of white. The fluff lies more than two feet thick, and despite being on cross-country skis, I occasionally sink through to my thighs on my trek across the desert floor. The struggle bathes me in perspiration.

Sunlight sparkles off the snow. Several miles before me the land heaves abruptly out of the desert in a saw-toothed wall 10,000 feet high—the eastern edge of the Sierra Nevada range. Streaks of gray rock, blasted clean of snow by high-altitude winds, break up the looming wall of white. Those gales, noiseless from where I am, blow films of white southward off the peaks of Baldwin, Morrison, McGee, and Laurel. The massive quartet gives the appearance of stately, veiled brides marching to the north.

In the midst of open country I ease into hot water, absolutely content. No house, no fellow human is within sight, nor any road. Surrounded by snow, I sit submerged to my chin in a thermal water pocket warmed by Earth's inner heat to over 100°F. Its clear waters are totally natural, and at this point, so am I, my clothes dangling from ski poles to dry in the sun. There is something blissful, almost fetal, about the contrasts, for I gaze on the frozen magnificence of one of the most beautiful mountain ranges in the world, while lying relaxed and warmed by the engine that created it.

The fires within the Earth that heat my pool also gave birth to this mountain range. Weeks earlier in Menlo Park, south of San Francisco, bearded, burly geologist Mike Diggles of the U.S. Geological Survey had described how the slow waltz

8

Rugged apostle of wilderness, naturalist John Muir views the Merced River in Yosemite, which became America's first large wilderness park at his fervent urging. Beginning in 1868, Muir wandered the Sierra Nevada, exulting in its beauty and proclaiming it "the Range of Light." His writings extolling the spirituality of wild, natural places helped inspire the national park movement and saved the giant sequoias from destruction. His passion for the outdoors led legions of urbanites into the mountain range.

9

Nature supplies the hot
water to soothe hiker Joe
Tichenor amid winter
snows in Long Valley at
the eastern edge of the
Sierra. Hot springs in the
valley bespeak the volcanism that still smolders
beneath the land. Colli-
sion of Earth's shifting
crustal plates millions of
years ago drove one plate
deep into the planet's
molten interior. Cooled
into granite and pushed
up by subterranean pres-
sures, the recycled rock
became what is perhaps
North America's most sto-
ried mountain range.

of Earth's crustal plates pushed up the Sierra Nevada. He knows the mountains on both a professional and personal level, for in addition to his full-time job studying their origins, he spends nearly every weekend hiking in them with a friend. "We can't get enough of the Sierra Nevada," he says, with a wide smile. "It's such a different world from the places where we work."

Construction of that world has grown clearer in recent decades with scientific acceptance of the theory of plate tectonics. Geologists now know that Earth's outer crust floats over the planet's molten interior in huge plates, like chunks of ice on a lake in spring breakup.

"Millions of years ago," Mike explained, "the Farallon and the larger Pacific plate—both west of today's California—and the North American plate, began moving toward one another. The Farallon came first, and being heavier, was forced under North America."

As the crust dove deep into Earth's mantle, intense heat melted it. Molten rock rose again toward the surface, and more of the plate slid down, insulating the underside of eastern California and Nevada from direct heat. Over a period of three million years, the molten rock cooled again and hardened into a solid mass called a batholith.

Eventually, nearly all the Farallon disappeared. It was now the Pacific plate's turn to bump against the North American plate. Unlike the Farallon, the Pacific plate was northbound. As it moved, it slid along the San Andreas Fault at the edge of the North American plate. Along this fault line, the plates, each miles thick, still move in fits and jerks that trigger California's infamous earthquakes.

With no more material plunging under North America, insulating the cooling mass that had been the leading edge of the Farallon, inner Earth's intense heat percolated upward. That rising heat pushed up the cooled mass—now turned to granite—like a giant soufflé. The rock riding the shoulders of the rising mass eroded in time, leaving granite spires commonly more than two miles high on the east side of the range and a gradual slope from 30 to 50 miles long to the west. During the last ice age, numerous glaciers passed over the still-rising granite, sometimes scouring it smooth, sometimes gouging wide valleys.

Lounging in my rustic spa, I am one of millions annually refreshed both physically and spiritually by the results of those cataclysmic events. As the afternoon wanes, I heave myself out of my winter womb reluctantly, dry off, dress, and follow my own deep ski tracks back to a roadway where my car awaits. As I pole through the snow, I make plans to downhill ski at Mammoth Mountain, just minutes away.

If anyone had dreamed a playground for the West Coast's largely office-bound population, it is difficult to imagine a better plan than this pushed-up, split-apart, and gouged-out landscape. Much of it is too rocky to plow, too steep to graze, too snowy to live on even half the year, and too beautiful to spoil—almost.

For decades the high country was ignored because of its seeming lack of productivity and for the rigors of living there. Now the desolation has become a destination, as crowded urbanites flee to the quiet and majesty of the Sierra. As bedroom communities and vacation homes sprout on the once-wild slopes, and fun seekers head for the hills, concern grows for the range that naturalist John Muir called "the most divinely beautiful of all the mountain-chains I have ever seen."

That beauty comes in many forms, for along its 400-mile length, from Lake Almanor in the north to Tehachapi Pass southeast of Bakersfield, the range offers an ever changing face.

In the far north, where the range was most heavily assaulted by glaciers, the highest summit, Sierra Buttes, reaches only 8,587 feet. More moisture falls at the northern end than the southern, due to a gap in the coastal range. Storm clouds off the Pacific pass through the Golden Gate strait at San Francisco and drop their cargo of moisture farther inland. The precipitation and the glacier-plowed richer soils nurture extensive stands of timber in the northern Sierra, the area of heaviest logging.

From Lake Tahoe south, the peaks are progressively larger, with dozens measuring over 13,000 feet high. Farther south near the town of Big Pine, a cluster of peaks over 14,000 feet reaches for the sky in the 150-mile stretch known as the High Sierra.

Lassen Peak
10,457 ft +

LASSEN
VOLCANIC
NAT. PARK

Susanville

36

36

89

Chester

Lake
Almanor

LASSEN
NAT.
FOREST

Honey
Lake

Indian
Creek

70

Pyramid
Lake

PLUMAS NATIONAL FOREST

Quincy

70

Middle Fk. Feather

N. Fk. Feather

Cascade Range

Sierra Buttes
8,587 ft

Downieville

N. Yuba

TAHOE NATIONAL FOREST

70

49

395

70

Reno

80

Truckee

Lake
Oroville

Feather
River

MALAKOFF DIGGINS
S.H.P.

S. Yuba

Nevada City

Truckee

TOIYABE
N.F.

DIAMOND PEAK SKI RESORT

50

99

Marysville

70

Yuba

Dutch Flat

49

80

DONNER
MEMORIAL
S.P.

N. Fk.

89

28

TAHOE NEVADA S.P.

Carson

41
95

Carson City

Bear

Auburn

S. Fk.

Lake
Tahoe

N E V A D A

Yerington

SUTTER'S MILL
MARSHALL GOLD DISCOVERY S.H.P.

505

5

Roseville

99

Coloma

Placerville

50

EMERALD BAY S.P.
DESOLATION
WILDERNESS

South Lake Tahoe

ELDORADO

HEAVENLY SKI RESORT

Stateline

Upper Truckee River

395

208

E. Walker

Walker
Lake

80

Sacramento

49

American River

NAT. FOR.

S. Fk.

Carson Pass
8,573 ft

09

W. Walker
River

95

Sacramento
River

Volcano

88

Ebbetts Pass
8,731 ft

Hawthorne

Sutter Creek

Jackson

4

TOIYABE

NATIONAL

FOREST

Makelumne

49

STANISLAUS

395

BODIE
S.H.P.

Angels Camp

NATIONAL

270

Conway Summit 8,138 ft

5

88

Stockton

108

FOREST

Mono
Lake

4

Sonora

Hetch Hetchy
Reservoir

YOSEMITE

120

Lee Vining

Benton Range

Benton

San Joaquin
River

120

NATIONAL

Tioga Pass
9,945 ft

INYO

6

White Mt. Peak
14,246 ft

To
San Francisco

205

580

Stanislaus

120

Yosemite Falls

El Portal

PARK

Yosemite Valley

NAT. FOR.
Mammoth
Lakes

Long
Valley

White Mountains Range

580

Tuolumne

DEVILS POSTPILE
NAT. MON.

MAMMOTH MT.
SKI RESORT

INYO

99

Merced

MARIPOSA
GROVE

Mt. Baldwin
12,690 ft

NAT.

Owens

FOR.

C A L I F O R N I A

49

Bishop

Merced

140

Inyo Mountains

41

SIERRA

S. Fk.

Big Pine

NATIONAL

North Palisade
14,242 ft

395

FOREST

KINGS CANYON

Paradise Valley

Cedar Grove

SEQUOIA
N. F.

Kings Canyon

San Joaquin

Fresno

MANZANAR N.H.S.

180

KINGS CANYON
NATIONAL PARK

Mt. Williamson +
14,375 ft

ALABAMA HILLS

Lone Pine

Moro Rock
6,725 ft

SEQUOIA

Mt. Whitney
14,494 ft

Owens
Lake
Bed

Kings

NATIONAL

INYO
NAT.
FOREST

190

198

PARK

To
Death Valley

Visalia

OLANCHA DUNES

99

Tulare
Lake Bed

SEQUOIA

1395

5

NATIONAL

S. Fk. Kern

FOREST

Kern

Kernville

178

Isabella Lake

Ridgecrest

395

V A L L E Y

LOS ANGELES AQUEDUCT

MOJAVE

58

Kern

Bakersfield

14

DESERT

Buena Vista
Lake Bed

58

Tehachapi

Tehachapi Mts.

Tehachapi Pass
3,800 ft

To Los Angeles

N

Point of Interest

National Park System

Pacific Crest Nat. Scenic Trail

0   40 mi

0   60 km

Inset map:

The Eastern
Escarpment
p. 140

NEVADA

Jewels of
the Sierra
p. 102

The Beckoning
Foothills
p. 40

CALIF

SIERRA NEVADA

Woods and Water
p. 72

Mostly above timberline, this southern portion includes more than 500 peaks above 12,000 feet, the attic of the Sierra Nevada.

The range's reputation for beauty began long before an urbanized population sought refuge here. In April 1776, Spanish Franciscan missionary Pedro Font looked eastward from a hill near today's San Francisco Bay and noted: "...we saw on the other side of the plain at a distance of some thirty leagues a great *Sierra Nevada*, white from the summit to the skirts...." In Spanish, *Sierra Nevada* means "snow-covered range," and although English eventually replaced Spanish as the dominant language in the area, the name stuck. If you want to mark yourself as an outsider, refer to the range as "the Sierras," which is wrong. *"Sierra* in Spanish is plural for 'mountain,'" explained Laurel Ames, a lifelong resident of Lake Tahoe. "You wouldn't say in English, 'mountainses,'" she scoffed. "They are 'the Sierra.'"

Somehow, the natural sculpturing undertaken by geologic events came together here in a way that is stunning to the eye, nurturing to the spirit, and rich in life. The region attracted humans long before the Spanish lifted their eyes to the hills. For centuries it harbored one of the most concentrated populations of Native Americans anywhere in North America. Sensibly residing in the foothills most of the year, they moved up the slopes in summer to escape the heat and to follow game. Acorns, seeds, waterfowl, fish, and fresh water abounded, and the hardiest hunters climbed high to take bighorn sheep.

On a bright day in February, researcher John Wehausen and I conducted our own kind of hunt, scanning the ridges above Owens Valley to estimate the dwindling numbers of the bighorn sheep. We paused along the way to browse on another staple of native diet: piñon nuts, better known to many as pine nuts, a key ingredient in making pesto. They hung in clumps on the fragrant piñon trees.

"The Indians climbed up here in the fall and gained weight by eating them," said John, as we popped the plump, succulent kernels into our mouths like candy. "The nuts are rich in protein and fat. They carried bundles of them downslope and made many things from them, but up here they just ate them the way we're doing.

FOLLOWING PAGES:
Oaks whisker the rolling
Sierra foothills, where
rich grasslands first
attracted Spanish cattle
ranchers. Several cen-
turies of grazing have
thinned the oak wood-

lands and altered the
native vegetation.
Urbanization brings
more concern as crowded
lowland cities spread onto
the slopes, cluttering
scenery and threatening
supplies of pure water.

I came up here last December and picked pounds of them to give away as Christmas presents."

Several groups of Native Americans—Miwok and Maidu Indians on the western slope, and Washo and Mono on the eastern—traded extensively in piñon nuts, acorns, shells, salt, and beads. Glasslike obsidian created by volcanic activity in Long Valley was worked into fine arrowheads that have been found among Indian artifacts thousands of miles away.

For centuries the height of the range and its abrupt eastern wall protected it from further human incursions. Spanish colonizers of Central and South America had sailed along the West Coast since 1542, but no inland exploration took place until 1769, when Gaspar de Portola's party rode north out of Mexico. By the early 19th century the Spaniards had established a line of forts and missions in the lowlands, but there seemed no reason to venture into the high country—except to pursue Indians who resisted conversion to Catholicism, sometimes fleeing the missions on the backs of Spanish horses.

The first recorded crossing of the Sierra was in 1827 by a small group led by mountain man Jedediah Smith. Looking for beaver streams, Smith and his party of trappers entered southern California through the Mojave Desert, but the *Americano* invaders were ordered out by the governor of what was then Spanish territory. Still on the lookout for beaver, they delayed their exit, wandering north while seeking a way to cross. They finally topped the ridge in a laborious, CONTINUED ON PAGE 34

A river turns to rain again as Yosemite Falls (left) begins its 2,425-foot drop to the floor of Yosemite Valley. During peak flow in spring, it creates its own wind and climate, forcing visitors to button up coats a quarter mile from its base. Highest waterfall in North America, the cataract first free-falls nearly 1,430 feet before thundering over rocks and falling unobstructed another 320 feet to the bottom, where it feeds into the Merced River. In a quieter mood, the Merced mirrors the ghostly face of El Capitan (opposite) in early morning. Rock climbers take days to scale the 3,500-foot sheer wall, sleeping in slings along the way. Dangerous? Yosemite park rangers report fewer accidents by trained climbers than by amateur scramblers who take too many chances throughout the park.

A fire scar in a giant sequoia fascinates a visitor to Sequoia National Park. Although fires aid reproduction of the sequoias by clearing brush and preparing soils for new seedlings, flames sometimes burn out cavities in their trunks.

Fire suppression over the past century has endangered adult trees by allowing the buildup of brush as fuel. The largest trees in the world can survive fire at their bases, but die when flames scorch crowns high overhead (below).

FOLLOWING PAGES: *Snow still patches the slopes of Mount Whitney as hikers head for the summit in August. Behind them looms the crest of the Sierra as they pass 13,000 feet in altitude. Each year, some 30,000 climb the tallest mountain in the lower*

48 states, requiring rangers to limit permits to 200 hikers per day in summer months. Foot traffic diminishes considerably when winter snows blanket Whitney, turning a tough one-day walk up and back into a technical alpine expedition that can take over a week.

Titanic rapids nearly submerge a kayaker competing with other whitewater specialists in the Kern River Festival. Good moves in high froth earn points from judges. Despite appearances, this competitor finished the run without incident.

Evening drops anchor on Emerald Bay in Lake Tahoe. A treasured enclave on a lake renowned for its beauty, the bay includes a small island at the southwest end, where wild geese nest. Sailboats and excursion paddle wheelers regularly cruise into the cove through its narrow entrance (top). Once a major means of transportation, watercraft ferried visitors to opposite shores before a road ringed the lake in 1913.

A sunset to close a two-reeler highlights the Alabama Hills (facing page), setting for dozens of feature films. For decades, moviemakers brought Hollywood to the nearby town of Lone Pine. A real-life drama played out over the briny waters of Mono Lake (below), where underground springs create mineral towers of tufa. As water was diverted from the lake's tributary streams, the lake dropped to critical levels. Court action now requires a gradual refilling.

FOLLOWING PAGES: *A garden of tumbleweeds grows at Olancha Dunes near the former Owens Lake. Mountains rising to more than 14,000 feet on both sides—the Sierra at left and the Inyo Mountains at right—make Owens the deepest valley in North America. Alkaloid soils now gleam white where steamboats once crossed 18-by-10-mile Owens Lake, once fed by mountain runoff. Diversion of water to Los Angeles in the 1920s dried up agriculture in the valley.*

CONTINUED FROM PAGE 15 hazardous crossing near Ebbetts Pass along what is now Highway 4, losing two horses and a mule in the deep snow.

More crossings occurred, from the east by trapper Joseph Walker and by explorer John C. Frémont. Word of the fertile, well-watered valleys of California spread to the "States," and immigrants in wagons began attempting crossings. The Donner party made its ill-fated attempt north of Lake Tahoe in October but was trapped by early snows, which entered them forever in the annals of gruesome history. By the time they were rescued the following spring, 47 of the original 87 had died, and the survivors had made it through by eating those who perished.

The difficulties posed by that formidable barrier caused most west-moving immigrants in the early 1840s to follow the Oregon Trail to the Northwest. California remained the sparsely populated province of vast cattle ranches and a few trading posts. Ironically, it was the rocks themselves, or rather the forces that created them, that led to a mass migration into the foothills of the Sierra Nevada. The discovery of gold in 1848 triggered one of the most sudden mass movements of humanity in history and ended California's long isolation from the rest of the civilized world.

Had Pedro Font, who named the Sierra Nevada, taken a closer look at the range as did another admiring visitor almost a century later, the mountains might have been known as *Sierra Lumina.* In a love affair with the mountains that would endure for the rest of his life, John Muir bestowed the range with a descriptive subtitle: "...after ten years of wandering and wondering in the heart of it, rejoicing in its glorious floods of light, the white beams of the morning streaming through the passes, the noonday radiance on the crystal rocks, the flush of the alpenglow, and the irised spray of countless waterfalls, it still seems above all others the Range of Light."

Not to mention a range of superlatives. The Sierra's 400-mile chain of unbroken relief makes it the longest solid block of mountains in the continental U.S. The Rocky Mountains may appear longer on a map, but they are cut through with gaps and stretches of lowlands. Despite the Sierra's length, all but a small segment on the eastern shore of Lake Tahoe lies within the state of California.

At 14,494 feet, Mount Whitney is the highest point in the lower 48 states. To the north of its peak, Kings Canyon lays claim to being the deepest canyon in North America, with walls cut through to a depth of 8,240 feet. Yosemite Falls cascades nearly half a mile, making it one of the highest falls in the world. Three other falls in Yosemite National Park also rank among the world's most impressive. Nothing else in the lower 48 states can match the Sierra's abrupt changes in topography. From the town of Lone Pine to the top of Mount Whitney the landscape rises from 3,733 feet to 14,494 feet, a vertical leap of more than 2 miles within a distance of 12 miles.

The Sierra claims the largest trees in the world, the auto-dwarfing sequoias of Sequoia National Park; some of the world's highest lakes; and some of the deepest snowpack outside arctic regions. The Sierra pushes high the moisture-laden air sweeping in off the Pacific that makes it past the coastal range; in cooling and condensing, clouds dump huge amounts of snow on the higher mountains. By mid-May 1998, with most of the nation witnessing explosions of emerald foliage, 14 feet of snow still covered roads at the highest elevations. I skied in both January and late May, and the ski season did not end at Mammoth Mountain until July.

The gradual melting of all that snow feeds cataracts that tumble down the western slope in a return to the Pacific. Every crease in the high mountains has its freshet, every ravine its plashing trout stream, every canyon its shimmering cascade, every valley its broad river. An abundance of water flows mostly west, a moving green and crystal treasury that dances, froths, and sparkles in the sunlight. Eleven major rivers flow west out of the Sierra, accounting for nearly half the runoff in all of California.

Despite all the minerals and trees that have been taken from the range, water is the most important resource to come out of it. Without water flowing from snow, the verdant, food-producing garden known as the Central Valley would be a barren desert. Rivers flowing off the east side water cities and farms in Nevada, and the Owens River system flowing east and south slakes the thirst of urbanites in Los Angeles.

In their pursuit of gravity, the rivers also carry tremendous loads of recreation. The South Fork of the American River east of Sacramento may be the most people-floated river west of the Rockies. Nearly 150,000 individuals either raft or kayak on the popular 21-mile stretch every year for the scenery and the thrill of negotiating rapids labeled "class three, maybe four" in difficulty.

"On a Saturday afternoon in the peak months of July and August, it's not unusual for a dozen craft to be within sight of each other at the principal bottleneck, a rapid known as Satan's Cesspool," said Corky Collier of California Outdoors, a trade association. "Nevertheless, a recent environmental impact study indicated a very high degree of satisfaction among participants. Of course, on non-peak days during the week, you might not be within sight of another boat."

Fun-seeking boaters also surge down other rivers draining the range—the Tuolumne, Merced, Yuba, and Kern. Six weeks in advance of the Memorial Day weekend, I called a half dozen hotels in Kernville, a jumping-off point for trips on the Kern River at the range's southern extremity. All of them required a three-night stay—which my schedule for the weekend didn't allow—and those not already fully booked were confident they would be. I ended up sleeping outside in a campground chock-a-block with recreational vehicles and tents.

If solid ground is your element and spring your favorite season, a gluttony of bucolic pleasure awaits. Spring in the Sierra lies within your reach six to eight months of the year. In January you can leave the ski slopes at higher altitudes and drive down in less than an hour to the lower slopes, to grass so dazzlingly green that it seems to dance before your eyes. In late July, when those lower slopes are golden from lack of rain, you can climb up to the cool, jade splendors of the high country and find a striking palette of wildflowers.

More than 30 million people live within half a day's drive of such seasonal variety and recreational opportunities. As one lifelong resident of the Sierra said to me, "The quintessential California weekend is skiing on Saturday and rafting the American River on Sunday."

Devotees of the Sierra claim it also has the finest mountain weather on earth, and they have some arguing points. Winters are wet but mild. Ninety-five percent of the moisture falls between October and May, and much of that as snow. Summers are dry—so dry that backpackers often leave their tents behind. Year-round, the sun shines seven days out of ten. Yosemite Valley in July promises a 97 percent chance of sunshine. The air is terrific, as visitor Mark Twain noted in the last century: "Three months of camp life on Lake Tahoe would restore an Egyptian mummy to his pristine vigor, and give him an appetite like an alligator."

So impressed was the humorist that he could only wax philosophical about life at higher elevations: "The air up there...," he wrote, "is very pure and fine, bracing and delicious. And why shouldn't it be?—it is the same the angels breathe."

This area the size of Vermont, New Hampshire, and Connecticut combined includes 10 state parks, 9 national forests, 19 national wilderness areas, 9 designated Wild and Scenic Rivers, and 3 national parks. The range is 70 percent public land and 30 percent privately owned.

Its most popular parks, Yosemite and Sequoia, are so heavily used that the National Park Service is currently revising methods of handling visitors. The General Management Plan for Yosemite Valley would wipe out some roads and campgrounds and transport people by bus in order to preserve the natural state of the park. Sequoia park officials survey the public for ideas on how to improve facilities, looking to ease traffic gridlock and eliminate commercial buildings clustered around the giant trees.

The parks have always been popular; now a growing population and rising frustration with urban living have drawn increasing numbers of people to nether parts of a range long accustomed to silence. This may be the most loved mountain range in the world. No one I spoke to disliked it, or was even neutral about it. Praise was frequent and effusive for the granite batholith that was hoisted out of the Earth's interior by volcanic hydraulics and eroded into a jumble of peaks, ravines, and rushing rivers.

"This is not just any mountain range," noted my sheep-counting friend, John Wehausen. "This is a unique place."

Two youngsters enjoy the timeless pleasures of a homemade swing near Coloma, California, in the foothills of the Sierra. The range that has become a mountain playground also beckons at lower elevations as a wholesome place to raise a family. Ancestors of these children have ranched here for more than a century. Now urbanites seeking a quieter life head for the hills, causing a flood of housing developments that threaten the tranquility of the region.

On the slopes above Lake Tahoe I shared a ski-lift chair one winter day with a young woman torn between a job she likes and a place for which she yearns. Shelly Palmer once lived in the Tahoe region, but the day we rose noiselessly through the frosted pines, she was on leave from a military post in the Midwest. "I love being in the military and I like the area where I'm stationed just fine," she said, "but I want to live here again! My current term is almost up and I'd like to reenlist, but I'm not sure I will. It's so beautiful here, and there's so much to do!"

One January I found myself watching the Super Bowl in a neighborhood bar in the Sierra foothills. A longtime traveling journalist, I know that a stranger's reception in a close-knit neighborhood establishment can range from curiosity to territorial hostility. Here I was welcomed as an honored guest by people who appeared relaxed and happy with their lot, though some spend hours commuting to jobs in the city.

Rory Low drives 45 minutes to a power company in Roseville at the edge of Sacramento, but the muscular lineman says it's worth the trip. "I do a lot of water skiing when I'm home, and a bunch of us go dirt biking together," he told me. "Sure, it's getting a little more crowded, but I can't blame people for moving out here. They just want the same thing I came for."

As more and more people seek joy in the Range of Light, the mountain peace erodes with the chatter of engines and the wheel tracks left on the land. So far the mountains have been able to absorb the numbers with solitude to spare, and even those concerned about the invasion understand the magnet that draws crowds.

"It's a wonderful place to live, and people are going to continue to move there as life becomes more and more unbearable in the cities," said Jay Watson of the Wilderness Society in San Francisco. "They are drawn to the clean air, clean water, recreational activities, and wonderful vistas—all just outside their door.

"Development in the range is going to continue. We just have to make sure we don't make the same mistakes in the Sierra that we've made elsewhere." ■

F O O T H I L L S

The Beckoning Foothills

PRECEDING PAGES:

Gentle slopes mark the western edge of the Sierra, where the range begins its gradual climb toward high peaks. Highway 49, named for the gold rush that peopled these hills, curves by the South Fork of the American River, upper left. The discovery of gold ended the isolation of a region long fenced off by its eastern escarpment.

T HE APPROACH TO THE SIERRA NEVADA FROM THE WEST IS AS gradual as the route from the east is abrupt. While the eastern heights thrust two miles skyward almost directly out of the desert, the western slope declines toward the Pacific at the rate of a hundred feet per mile.

The range begins with the foothills, which extend from California's Central Valley to about 2,000 feet in the north and to about 5,000 feet in the south, a rolling landscape covered by oak woodlands, thick brush known as chaparral, and grass. Compared with the awesome rock abutments and sheer cliffs of the eastern heights, this is a gentle, hospitable land. Beef cattle graze on the hillsides; small towns cluster between the hills. Until the mid-19th century, the only human inhabitants were Native Americans, decades after Lewis and Clark had shown the way to the West Coast.

Little more than 150 years ago, west of the Sierra, a few Spanish ranchers fattened cattle on the valley grasslands, and Catholic missions harvested heathen souls. Mexico ceded California to the U.S. in 1848, but few in the young nation saw any reason to cross the cold, rocky barrier. Observed by few but Native Americans, snow fell in the high country, melted in the warmer months, and the runoff tumbled toward lower ground. With it came another substance that would open the floodgates of humanity to the Far West.

As the molten material deep underground slowly cooled into the building blocks of the Sierra, among the materials that solidified were quartz and gold. While still fluid, they oozed into cracks in the hardened granite, sometimes together, forming light-colored veins. After the granite rose to form the Sierra, frost, glaciers, and water erosion slowly gnawed at the mountains, and fragments of gold washed downstream. Much heavier than most rock, it settled into riffles and sandbars of the rushing streams.

On the morning of January 24, 1848, James Marshall walked near the lumber mill he was building for Swiss immigrant and entrepreneur John Sutter, in a pleasant valley the Native Americans called "Cullomah" (now Coloma), east of today's Sacramento. Water from the swift-flowing South Fork of the American River had been detoured through a hand-dug mill-

The mill that brought millions has been reconstructed along the South Fork of the American River at Coloma, using original plans drawn by its builder, James Marshall. In the millrace that returned diverted water to the river, Marshall spied a shining fleck and verified with mill owner John Sutter that it was gold. The resulting stampede to the West Coast changed U.S. history and ruined the two men responsible. Visitors can now watch the saw cut planks and pan for gold.

race to turn a wheel that would power a log-cutting blade. As Marshall checked the race for depth, he noticed something glinting under the water. Retrieving it, he hammered it with a rock and noted its softness, a characteristic of gold.

The discovery may not have been a total accident; Marshall was known to suspect there might be gold in the river, and he is believed to have prospected occasionally in search of it. His own recollection of relating the discovery minutes later to his friend William Scott sounds as if they had previously discussed the possibility:

"I have found it."

"What is it?" inquired Scott.

"Gold," I answered.

"Oh no," returned Scott, "it can't be."

I replied positively, "I know it to be nothing else."

When Marshall showed the flake and other samples to his partner, John Sutter wanted to keep it quiet. He dreamed of an agricultural empire with a gristmill for making flour in addition to the sawmill cutting slab lumber, and he worried that excitement over gold would make it difficult to hire workers. Sutter and Marshall swore their mill workers to silence, but word trickled out. What came to be known as the gold rush reportedly began when a businessman named Sam Brannan walked the streets of San Francisco waving a bottle of gold dust and yelling, "Gold! Gold! Gold from the American River!"

San Francisco emptied as men streamed to the countryside. Sailors deserted their ships, leaving them nodding uselessly in the harbor. Walter Colton, the town administrator of Monterey, wrote: "The blacksmith dropped his hammer, the carpenter his plane, the mason his trowel, the farmer his sickle, the baker his loaf.... All were off to the mines...."

By 1849 dreams of wealth were drawing "forty-niners" from all over the world. They came from the eastern United States, from Central and South America, from Europe, Australia, India, the Malay Peninsula, and the South Seas. Young Chinese mortgaged their futures and sailed across the Pacific to the California they knew as *Gum Shan*—Gold Mountain. The Sierra's isolation ended in what has been called the greatest human migration in history. In two years, California's non-Indian population went from some 14,000 to 100,000, and in two more years it had jumped to 250,000.

The Native Americans in the region were virtually wiped out, killed by diseases brought by the newcomers and by violence bred of greed and distrust of all red men. A chief of the Nisenan tribe is reported to have said, "The spirit that owns the yellow metal is a bad spirit. It will drive you crazy if you possess it."

If a single word must be used to describe the gold rush, "crazy" is as good as any. Prospectors spread from the American River to the Sacramento and the San Joaquin, then to all rivers and streams along the western foothills. Greed, backbreaking work, and an oversupply of testosterone in the nearly all-male camps bred a bawdy lifestyle. Miner Lucius Fairchild, who would later become a Wisconsin Supreme Court justice, wrote to a friend back home: "Gambling, drinking, and houses of ill fame are the chief amusements of this county." Lacking women, men danced with each other, the "females" identified by a bandanna tied on one arm.

A few gained fortune and fame. Leland Stanford, a small-time merchant near Sacramento, became rich in the goldfields and later governor of California, a U.S. senator, and the founder of a university. George Hearst, father of newspaper magnate William Randolph Hearst, enhanced the family's coffers with his Sheep Ranch Gold Mine.

Others profited handsomely. Nine men took out gold amounting to $8,000 each from a place called Bidwell's Bar, sold their claim for another $12,000 each, and returned East. Though others may have improved on their own wages, expenses skyrocketed as well. Bread sold at $2 a pound, butter at $6. A bottle of ale went for $8, and a box of sardines for $16. Desperate to set up field camps and haul in their gold, miners paid $20 for a shovel and $100 for a blanket.

Prostitutes struck a mother lode of lust. One admitted making $50,000 and said she could have doubled it, had she the stamina. A black woman named Mary Ellen "Mammy" Pleasant set up a chain of brothels and became a wealthy advocate for civil rights, at one point handing abolitionist John Brown $30,000 to finance his ill-fated raid on the federal arsenal at Harper's Ferry, Virginia, now in West Virginia.

By 1853, the free-for-all was over. Gold mining would continue for many years, even though the easy pickings from the streams were gone. In the century after Marshall's discovery, nearly 2.5 billion dollars in gold was taken from the foothills of the Sierra Nevada, giving California the nickname of the Golden State.

Neither John Sutter, whose lumber mill unearthed the treasure, nor James Marshall, who found the first nuggets, profited from the excitement. Sutter's workers deserted to look for gold, speculators swindled him out of his lands, forty-niners stole his livestock for food, and a vagrant ex-soldier burned down his home. Marshall failed to find much gold despite his head start, and in his bitterness drank away what little money he had.

Although they died in poverty, both men live on in a wealth of fame. Thousands returned to Coloma on January 24, 1998, for observance of the 150th anniversary of the discovery of gold. Sutter's Mill, rebuilt from the original plans drawn by Marshall, again sawed planks off logs, to the delight of crowds. The Coloma museum displayed Marshall's nugget that started it all, a flattened piece of gold the size of half a cornflake, on loan from the Smithsonian Institution.

A mixture of modern tourists and characters lifted out of the mid-1800s strolled the grounds. Bearded men in stained suits of buckskin lectured to anyone who wanted to learn how to prime a flintlock or cure a beaver pelt. Against a backdrop of white canvas tents, women in long dresses stirred iron pots simmering over slow-burning fires. The romance of the gold rush has spawned a fascination with reenactments.

Bill Brown could have walked into a mining camp in 1848 without drawing a second look at his wide-brimmed hat or handmade boots. Nineteenth century lore spills from him like tall tales from a mountain man. "Buckskin soaked in deer brains breathes better, so it's not so hot to wear," he told me, fingering his outfit. A comment on his hat elicited a sartorial tidbit: "Ever notice how so many men in those early photographs wore their brims turned up? Makes no sense, and I don't think it was common practice. A friend of mine studied old pictures and found that all the people in the background had the brim turned down. He concluded that those early photographers asked that brims be turned up so faces wouldn't be shaded."

While eating at an outdoor table, I asked the woman across from me in period dress and lace-up boots what brought her to the sesquicentennial. Deborah McClatchy unreeled a true tale of her great-great-grandfather's search for gold. In 1849 James McClatchy boarded a ship on the East Coast and sailed to Panama. From there he trekked across the isthmus, then boarded a second ship, which sank off Mazatlan, Mexico. One of 26 survivors who swam ashore, he walked to San Diego while surviving on toads, rattlesnakes, and berries, then made it to the foothills, where he found enough gold to help establish the *Sacramento Bee*.

Deborah now honors that history by singing songs of the era. I followed her into the performance tent, where she played banjo and belted out foot-tapping tunes of the gold rush:

Roll boys roll, to Californ-I-O,
There's plenty of gold,
So I've been told,
On the banks of the Sacramento.

Descendants of the forty-niners still live in the foothills, among all the newcomers who stake claims to ranchettes and work at computers in coastal cities. In many restaurants you can still buy pasties, the meat-and-potato-pie legacy of miners from Cornwall. Chinese immigrants ushered "China-town" into the American lexicon as they clustered in major cities, but the Chinese influence can still be seen in the restaurants and cleaning establishments of small towns as well. Sutter Creek, some 30 miles south of Coloma, has been holding its annual Italian Picnic Parade for a century, in tribute to Italians who settled there.

This is festival country, with a fete or two or three for every community. Besides the Italian Picnic Parade, Sutter Creek has also started a hot air balloon festival because, as one of the organizers, Wendy Woolrich, told me, "Dave Gebauer suggested it and the rest of us thought it was a wonderful idea. Besides, our little airport where it's held is a jewel, and it's underused."

Wendy, the owner of a gift shop called "Cabbage Rose," is a member of the Sutter Creek Business and Professional Association, which plans festivals, drawing business to the area. Year-round, a festival somewhere awaits visitors to the foothills—the Winterfest at Chester in February, the storytelling festival in Mariposa in March, the Wild West Stampede in Auburn in April, a Native American powwow in Tehachapi in June, a fiddlers contest in Placerville in December. Most draw on the area's gold rush history.

A few miles from Coloma a family still lives the life of ancestors drawn to the foothills by gold. Cheri Little's great-grandfather William Bacchi came from the Swiss-Italian border in 1850. When gold eluded him, he turned to what he knew—buying some cows, planting grapes, and making cheese and wine to sell. He homesteaded 160 acres, bought more, and his descendants did the same until Bacchi land totaled 10,000 acres. The federal government took some of the land in forced sales for public works projects, but ranching has continued in the family for 150 years.

Cheri and her husband, Paul Little, in partnership with Cheri's brother Chuck Bacchi, and his wife, Judy, seasonally graze their beef cattle in the Coloma area and the high country. By the end of May, grasses shrivel into dry stems in the California foothills. Every cow, bull, and calf must be loaded onto trucks for the trip to the mountains—either Forest Service land in the Sierra or to Bacchi land 350 miles north in Oregon—where they will graze until rounded up and trucked back in October and November.

We arose at 4 a.m. for a quick breakfast before saddling horses in the dark to herd cattle into the trucks. They put me on a mount named Bud, known for his patience with children and with dudes who don't wear spurs. Dew still glistened on the grass as Cheri, Chuck, and I herded Hereford cows and their calves toward the chutes, where the hired trucks stood ready.

This much was pleasant, for me at least—I did not do it every day and had no stake in the outcome. A good horse beneath me, the whitefaces ambling dutifully along a fence line, the air clear and the green hills stretching away under blue skies. Near the chutes where we separated the cattle into loadable groups, a calf tried to join the wrong family. I pointed Bud toward it and touched him with my heels. Ears forward, he saw what was needed and moved briskly to cut the maverick back where he belonged. "Good move!" said Cheri in approval.

To those of us imbued with a romantic image of cowboys, the Littles and Bacchis live colorful lives, wearing chaps over jeans, herding and roping from cow-savvy horses, their spurs ringing on the floor of the ancestral ranch house. The two families would scoff at that image, for they know the reality of long hours in the saddle, of repairing fences and doctoring livestock, of dismounting to urge kicking, bawling, butting 400-pound calves and 1,000-pound cows through mud and manure toward suspicious-looking vehicles that every animal seeks to avoid. Paul Little had to lay off the heavy work this day because his horse had fallen backward as he rode it up a steep bank the day before, bruising him painfully. This is no trail ride on drowsy nags, no gentle communion with the wide-open spaces. It's a tough life, requiring tough people, and the Littles and Bacchis are devoted to it. Their teenage children work alongside them when not in school; challenged on the range, the children excel in athletics.

"Paul and I never wanted to do anything but ranch," said Cheri, as we drove around the vast pastures of El Dorado County where they winter their livestock. "My whole life has been owning land and improving it."

No family of provincial outlanders, they are keenly aware of changes happening around them. Chuck Bacchi worked in the California Legislature for several years and served as assistant to the governor of Guam before returning to the home property. Paul and Cheri's coffee table is littered with periodicals, and discussions over lunch included the latest best-selling books.

Now home owners seeking a piece of rural ambiance threaten their way of life. The family rents most of the land their cattle graze, and the landowners can make much more money selling off building lots than providing grass for cattle. Not far past the loading chutes, suburbia suddenly appears on a hillside. "The man who sold this ranch got $5,000 an acre," said Cheri. "We can't afford to pay that kind of money to graze cattle on it. So developers buy it and build houses. Buyers come for the view, but if they keep building houses, there won't be any view left!"

The newcomers require schools, police, and fire protection, services that raise taxes on all property owners including the ranchers, whose margins of profit on thousands of acres are already thin.

"We're caught in a squeeze," said Chuck Bacchi, as we sat around a table loaded with hearty ranch fare—chicken and beef roasted on an outdoor grill and bowls of vegetables. "The government will grant us a conservation easement, which gives us tax advantages and means the land can only be sold for ranching purposes. But who can say that heirs will want to ranch? And you don't want to leave them land that has been devalued."

The gold rush of the 19th century has been replaced by the "view rush" of the 20th and 21st. Urbanites head for the hills, seeking a better quality of life than seems possible anymore in the cities. Clint Walker, who played the strong, silent type as Cheyenne Bodie on television in the 1950s and 60s, retreated to a small acreage near Nevada City at the northern end of the gold corridor.

"I wanted a place where the air was clear, the sky was blue, the water tasted good, and I could have a little elbow room," he drawled in the same congenial baritone that brooked no nonsense from villains for eight years on the television series *Cheyenne*.

Sometimes confrontations between urbanite and rancher take on the look of cattleman-sheepman feuds of the Old West that Walker negotiated in his TV role. Said Paul Little of his new neighbors, "They cut our fences so they can get their four-wheelers on our land, poach, leave trash, help themselves to firewood, and their dogs pull down a calf every now and then."

Farther south at Sonora, where some newcomers commute nearly two hours daily to jobs in the San Francisco Bay area, gunfire killed a cow grazing on federal land. Cattleman's Association member Sherri Brennan said, "I think ranchers and nonranchers need to sit down and talk about their differences and find common ground."

For all the residential invasion, the foothills possess open country and small-town charms that draw visitors in addition to permanent residents. A drive along Highway 49, named for the gold rush, still offers vistas of rolling, oak-studded hills, and nearly every old mining town plays on its visual history. The past is present in a weathered miner's cabin, in the assay-office-turned boutique, in high storefronts with second-story balconies that cover sidewalks against winter rains. Downieville, Nevada City, Jackson, and Sutter Creek all retain a 19th century flavor to mine gold from tourist pockets.

An admirer of old hotels, I gravitated often to the Cary House Hotel in Placerville, once known as Hangtown for the swift justice incurred there. Over a 20-year period, local entrepreneur Doug Milton renovated the old hotel with ceiling fans in the lobby, stained-glass windows that depict aspects of local history, and provocative red wing-backed chairs that suggest a long-gowned entertainer could swish down the grand staircase at any moment, sliding a gloved hand along the dark wood banister. The room clerk sits in a metal cage, a reminder of the days Wells Fargo used the hotel as a pickup point for silver and gold bullion destined for the San Francisco mint. Today it hides computers, the modern equivalent of the rotating sign-in book. In September 1997, a partnership of 13 local boosters bought the hotel and gave each of the three floors of guest rooms separate themes—wine country, local gold mines, and famous area residents. The feeling is of yesteryear with all the modern conveniences.

Placerville lies some 40 miles east of Sacramento, and commuters now speed to bedroom communities on the Route 50 freeway. David Jones, who moved to Placerville in 1988 to grow award-winning wine grapes from the rich volcanic soils, worries about the influx. "Water is key to everything," says the former USGS geologist, "and there won't be enough to go around if we have uncontrolled development."

Houses have also infiltrated the hills around little Dutch Flat just off Interstate 80 between Sacramento and Reno, Nevada, but the town itself

Prospecting for happiness, Herb Schotz lives alone in a tiny pole-and -plastic shack while seeking gold in Bear River. "Hermit Herb, a river rat" he calls himself in the Kiplingesque poetry he writes in his notebook for diversion. For the past decade he has shoveled sand into a sluice box to capture "color" overlooked by his predecessors a century and a half ago. Hobbyists and vacationers still scour California streams, but the easy pickings played out long ago. Herb says his hard work barely covers expenses, but earns him a wealth of personal peace.

remains an enclave of small, scattered Victorian houses. "There's no sewage system, and some of the lots that remain are too small to install a septic," said local historian Russell Towle.

Some people would like to see it stay that way, a quiet village with a tiny post office and a general store. Towle feels that a little tourist trade would create a reason for saving the few trails and scenic wonders that remain, including a 2,400-foot "lover's leap" that he said many locals don't even know about. "I don't want to see mini-malls and strip development," said Towle, "but the community might benefit from more people knowing what we have here."

For all the concern about the gradual effects of the gold rush, a few miles outside Dutch Flat I visited a throwback to that earlier era. Following directions from locals, I walked down Bear River and hallooed the camp of Herb Schotz, a modern placer miner. For a decade he has camped on rugged, uninhabited land at a bend of the Bear, scrabbling gold dust from the riverbanks. His beard flared wildly and his hair seemed a stranger to combs, but he brimmed with a quiet vitality and enthusiasm for a life in the wild.

Every day he starts up a lawn-mower-size engine that pumps water from the stream into a one-man sluice box. As he shovels sand and gravel into the riffled sluice, water washes away most silt and lighter materials, leaving black sand and gold dust—what there is of it —on the bottom.

After an hour of shoveling, he shut off the engine and emptied the contents of the sluice into a gold-mining pan. He carefully swished out water and rocks until pay dirt finally showed in one corner. Perhaps an eighth of a teaspoon. Most years, Herb says, he clears about $1,800 after expenses.

Some people wouldn't call it a living, he offered, but after a second failed marriage and an industrial accident that he says made him unemployable, he decided to work out his days alone on the river. In a few years the 61-year-old plans to sell his last vial of gold dust and retire in Florida, where he'll build a boat and live on Social Security. In the meantime, he says, "I've learned a lot about myself."

Perhaps the lack of companionship has made him forget the volume of speech required for conversation, for even in his 10-by-10 pole-and-plastic shelter I had to lean forward to catch his words above the murmur of the creek. Passages of the Kiplingesque poetry he composes were offered in answer to many of my questions. When I asked him why he chose this life, he smiled and recited from his "Evening in the Mining Camp." The words would resonate well with many who have sought the beauty of the Sierra foothills, both yesterday and today:

> No suits for me, no fancy car,
> I've left that all behind.
> I only work for basics now
> and gained my peace of mind. ∎

FOLLOWING PAGES:
Playing ewes to orphaned lambs, 13-year-old Matthew Little and his cousin Rachel Bacchi, 5, offer bottled milk. Their great-great-grandfather, William Bacchi, came to the gold fields from Switzerland in 1850, part of a massive immigration from around the globe. When fortune eluded him, he turned to ranching, a way of life still honored by his descendants.

Young buckaroos clutch their hats for the national anthem at the Mother Lode Roundup and Rodeo in Sonora. Entered in the junior division, they compete in roping calves and riding miniature bulls in a rodeo that dates back to 1918. Festivals and

events in the small communities scattered along the foothills honor local traditions while also attracting city dwellers seeking entertainment in the countryside. At the Calaveras County Fair at Angels Camp, a 4-H

Club member cuddles a rabbit (above, left). A hopper of another sort at Angels Camp launched the career of author and humorist Mark Twain when he wrote of a jumping frog contest held there in the 1860s.

FOLLOWING PAGES:
*Cupboard for birds, a
rotting oak dotted with
holes provides food storage
for acorn woodpeckers.
Spring greens the lowlands,
while snow still drapes the
giant trees higher up.*

Buttering a woodland floor, California poppies surround oaks along Highway 49 near Auburn. Spring in the Sierra can be followed for half a year because of the gradual increase in elevation from the foothills to mountain peaks. In its season, a spider explores a Sierra layia in the foothills. A last flush of spring flowers adorns high meadows as alpine snows melt, often in July, after lowland hills have turned brown again.

59

"The Whopper," they call the clump (opposite) found in the Sixteen-To-One gold mine northwest of Lake Tahoe. Acid washed out surrounding rock and left the honey-combed chunk, valued as a novelty at $225,000. "It's kind of the company mascot," said a mine employee. Used to more modest finds, Douglas Mead and Sheila Long-necker (below) have worked mine tailings for 20 years. Their average annual findings total less than The Whopper's 141 troy ounces.

FOLLOWING PAGES: *Yesterday's industry rusts on a hillside near Jackson, California, seen through the spokes of a tailings wheel. Former owners of the Kennedy Gold Mine had to build the 58-foot wheel to elevate tailings to a retaining dam after mine residue began dam-aging farmlands down-stream. Pulleys in the dis-tant tower lowered men and mules as deep as a mile below ground to send up gold valued at $34.3 million. The mine closed in 1942. A local foundation now offers tours, with funds going to historic restoration.*

PRECEDING PAGES: *Young sourdoughs try their luck panning at a trough salted with gold dust and tiny flakes at Coloma. In early 1998, two days of reenactments near Sutter's Mill marked the 150th anniversary of the discovery of gold in California. Some 16,000 attendees could also pan the American River, hear tall tales from mountain men, and view the original gold flake found nearby, on loan from the Smithsonian Institution.*

A fiddler in old-time dress waits backstage with his group (opposite) before performing gold camp songs at the sesquicentennial celebration of the discovery that peopled California. The gold rush spawned its own folk music and expressions. Today's stock market terms "bull" and "bear" derive from animal fights staged for the amusement of miners; the bull gored upward, the bear tried to drag the bull down. Dressed in 1850s clothing (above), eighth graders from Gold Trail School in nearby Placerville romp in a dance of yesteryear.

Auto headlights blaze a modern trail in the historic district of Angels Camp. Like many an old mining town in the gold rush area, the one made famous by Mark Twain's jumping frog tale retains a frontier appearance to draw well-heeled outsiders. Assay-offices-turned-boutiques now receive currency from tourist pockets. Porches and balconies, sometimes even board sidewalks, lead the nostalgic into gift shops and restaurants that recall the past.

The dome and statuary of the Auburn courthouse gleam in the morning sun. Gold brought people to this mining town in the foothills, but the rush was over well before the courthouse was completed in 1894. Gen. George A. Custer, whose dreams fell short against the Sioux, takes a suction-cupped arrow in a bar in Volcano, California (above). Native Americans won few victories as gold seekers invaded, driving tribes virtually into extinction.

WOODS AND WA

TER

*Dark forest just before
dawn surrounds gleaming
Donner Lake, named for
immigrants trapped here
by deep snow in 1846.
Survivors made it through
winter by cannibalizing
those who perished. Today,
sheltering woods and
mountain waters draw
millions of visitors
throughout the year.*

W E USUALLY THINK OF EUROPE AS THE PLACE TO ADMIRE GREAT
houses of worship, but you can stand amid cathedrals in the Sierra. The huge
trees that grow there command the same kind of reverence felt when gazing
at a soaring monument to God. Whether or not you accept the tenets of
religion is irrelevant. In both church and forest, the majesty stuns you to
silence, and the details of construction stagger the imagination.

We also associate great cities with elaborate fountains, where crowds
gather to watch the dance of water and be cooled by the mist. Water lovers
gather as well at the many falls and rapids of the Sierra, where torrents fight
past boulders in a great, thundering, rainbow-making rush.

Gold may have drawn people to the Sierra, but woods and water keep
visitors coming by the millions every year. In the ample snows of winter
they ascend for some of the best skiing in the world. In California's rain-
less summers they escape from the parched lowlands to take in the cool
silence of the forests and the hundreds of tumbling streams.

The conifer forests of the Sierra Nevada generally stretch from an elevation of 2,000 feet in the north and 5,000 feet in the south on up to the
bare rock above timberline, although stands may be found as low as 1,200
feet in the north and as high as 10,000 feet in the south. The crest of the
range divides some species; piñon pines are common on the east side but
seldom found on the west, while for black oak, the reverse is true.

On the long western slope, ponderosa pine and white fir dominate
between 3,000 and 7,000 feet. Mixed among them may be incense cedar,
sugar pine, and black oak. Forests on the western slope may include Douglas fir, Jeffrey pine, and the largest trees on Earth—the giant sequoias. Red
fir and lodgepole pine thrive at higher altitudes. Altogether, 25 species of
conifer and 41 species of hardwoods grow in the range, plus numerous
shrubs. They act as sponges that soak up water and release it slowly, preventing erosion and providing a year-round flow down the slopes.

We see a different forest than the Native Americans knew. They walked
in brush-free woods under a high canopy. Periodic fires of low intensity

Towering over a rustic
museum building, this
sequoia is just one of more
than 200 giants protected
in Mariposa Grove
in Yosemite National
Park. Another tree in the
grove, the "Grizzly
Giant," is thought to be
2,700 years of age, mak-
ing it one of the most
venerable sequoias.

swept through, clearing brush and nurturing new growth for wildlife while leaving the large trees unharmed. Late in the 19th century John Muir could still note: "The inviting openness of the Sierra woods is one of their most distinguishing characteristics. The trees of all the species stand more or less apart in groves, or in small irregular groups, enabling one to find a way nearly everywhere, along sunny colonnades and through openings that have a smooth, park-like surface, strewn with brown needles and burrs...."

More than a century later, I have known that walk through a "park-like surface," but only in parks. Hiking in Kings Canyon in the southern part of the range, I strode through tall shafts of pine on ground springy with needles. I paused at one giant, a ponderosa in rich canyon soil with a girth that defied embrace. Placing my feet snug against the bole, I took 18 heel-to-toe steps around its circumference.

Elsewhere, logging has removed most of the very large pines. Young trees now replace them, but the difference between standing in an old forest and a new one is that of being among elder statesmen or hanging out with teenagers— the former erect and dignified, the latter jockeying for space and spotlight.

Some think the dignity of aged trees and powerful falling waters rubs off on us. Driving in the far northern, heavily wooded end of the Sierra, I rounded a curve to spy the perfect combination of noble trees and tumbling water. Indian Creek fought its way past high boulders and layers of shale, along river banks lined with tall, straight yellow pines. I pulled over to let my senses feast on the sights and sounds of raw water power and the elegance of century-old living giants.

A van pulled over almost simultaneously and out stepped two young women equipped with lunch. Boulder-hopping to a spot away from the road and nearer the water, they unfolded a meal of pasta salad, chilled white wine, and fresh strawberries.

"I love this spot; I've known it for years," said Traci Wierman, a teacher in Redding, California. "The water and the trees are awesome, and the rocks near the river remind me of a Japanese garden. See the patches of lupine, and the stumpy, angular trees growing out of the rocks?"

So they stop here occasionally to enjoy the view, I observed, declining the offer of a yogurt-dipped strawberry.

"I think it's important for people to get back in touch with the outdoors," said Traci's companion, Laurie Salles. "This is probably the first time in history that people have felt they can get along without nature."

"But they can't really get along without places like this," said Traci above the thunder of river current. "You need them for mental health."

The Sierra is filling with people seeking the same therapy. I headed north to Lake Almanor, bought lunch, and drove for miles along the shore looking for an opening where I could eat and look over this quieter water, but vacation homes crowded the shore. Two dozen private resorts and campgrounds also surround the 52-square-mile lake. Although logging remains an important industry in Plumas County—Collins Pine, a timber-cutting and processing company at nearby Chester, employs 200 people—bait shops and restaurants now line the streets.

"Recreation now drives our economy," said Jim Roscoe, president of the local chamber of commerce. "Timber used to be the solid base, with recreation the icing on the cake. Now the timbering has been cut in half, but we're still a healthy community, with retirees who spend half a year here and tourists who come to fish."

Perhaps nowhere in the Sierra do woods, water, and fun come together better than at Lake Tahoe. Some would expand that superlative, as Samuel Clemens did, to include the world. Not yet known as Mark Twain when he visited in 1861, he later wrote of the "...noble sheet of blue water...walled in by a rim of snow-clad mountain peaks....I thought it must surely be the fairest picture the whole earth affords." Long before the arrival of white visitors, the Washo Indians considered it sacred and gathered at *da ow a ga*, "the edge of the lake," and perhaps gave Tahoe its name.

The first non-natives passing through the area had personal wealth in mind—the silver of the Comstock Lode discovered a few miles to the east. Loggers in the mid-19th century leveled forests around the lake to provide timbers for the mines, building roads that brought more visitors. By the turn of the century, luxury hotels had sprouted, and after World War II visitors began coming in droves for the views, the gambling at the proliferating casinos, and eventually, for skiing on the surrounding mountains.

This virgin beauty has been blemished by the onslaught, with subdivisions and high-rises crowding its shores and silt clouding waters that once boasted clarity to over 100 feet, now down to 74. A beauty the lake remains nevertheless, drawing millions every year, most arriving on the seven roads that lead into the basin.

A world traveler for the National Geographic for a quarter century, I have feasted on many pleasing views, but few that fit the description "breathtaking." Lake Tahoe can be breathtaking, eye-widening, and mind-numbing, if seen from the right perspective. For me it was from the top of the first ski lift at the ski resort with the less-than-modest name of "Heavenly."

Before me spread an inland sea extending 22 by 12 miles, with waters the color of sapphire. The rich blue stems from its clarity and depth, at 1,645 feet the continent's third deepest lake. Tahoe had slumped as the rest of the Sierra rose, and lava dammed the lower end to let the hole fill with snowmelt. I stared in wonder. Sun-brightened snow surrounded the lake completely and deepened the blue, like a sapphire spotlighted in a nest of cotton. I should have enjoyed the view longer, but I had planned a busy schedule. In the morning I skied at Heavenly; in the afternoon I would sail on the lake. Three pleasures, if you count my visit to a casino that night.

It was nearly mid-May, and the last day of Heavenly's ski season. A few bare spots on the slope facing the lake made me dubious about the prospects, but a lift operator assured me that there was plenty of good skiing on the California side. Heavenly begins in Nevada, but the back side of the first ridge takes you into California, and sure enough, a couple of thousand feet above the lake the snow lay deep and inviting. I joined hundreds of others in gleeful runs down well-groomed trails. Blue sky, bright sun, crisp air, clean snow, great scenery, and the exhilaration of downhill speed—the combination that draws tens of thousands a year to Tahoe's 15 major ski resorts. Six of the largest sold 3.2 million lift tickets in the 1997-98 season.

After a ten-minute drive from the ski lodge, I pulled into a marina where Jim Hildinger waited with his 27-foot sailboat. A brisk wind rippled the water, skies were clear, and temperatures were merely invigorating, but only one other white sail was visible in the distance. "That's why I sail only from October to June," said Jim as we cast off. "It gets too crowded in summer."

Still impressed by the view from atop Heavenly, I related my astonishment at the palette of deep blue against snowy mountains, bordered by a narrow band of green where they met at water's edge.

"It's when you look down into the depths that Tahoe's problems become apparent. Thirty years ago one could see a 12-inch white dinner plate at 110 feet. Today that clarity has been reduced to about 74 feet, and we lose about 3 feet each year. This is due to the growth of algae that feed on nutrients and phosphates that are carried into the lake by rivers and streams."

A lifelong resident of Tahoe, the retired music teacher eyes development around the lake with bitterness. "Nature is unforgiving; when you lose it, it's gone. I'm not very optimistic about what's happening."

It's hard to stay a pessimist on a crystal day with Lake Tahoe virtually to yourself. A smile crept across his face as we headed into Emerald Bay, a mountain-ringed fjord with a little island at the southwest end. "The most photographed place on the lake, maybe in the whole Sierra," he said.

The paddle wheeler *Tahoe Queen* churned by us with a load of sightseers, like a relic from a past when ferries were the main way of reaching distant shores. The Rim of the Lake Road was finished in 1913, and some would say that it signaled the decline in Tahoe's beauty. Still, the beauty that remains is in a class by itself. The forested slopes, the stalwart peaks, the vast expanse of blue keep Jim Hildinger sailing four days out of seven in those months when water traffic wanes.

"I've sailed on the ocean, but nothing compares with this," he said as, hand on the tiller, he looked up the mast to check the wind direction. Sailing on Tahoe keeps a mariner on his toes, he admitted, for the uncertain winds sweeping off the heights left us slack one moment and heeling over to the gunwales the next. Capsizing, I hoped, was not on my agenda, for while Tahoe never freezes, its waters are cold enough in

Tongues flying, sled dogs strain in the traces as a musher urges them on in a race in Chester, California. Although sled dogs saw little historic use in the Sierra, Chester began sponsoring the event 15 years ago as a winter diversion and to bring in business. Teams from California, Oregon, Washington, and Colorado compete for cash prizes. Summertime recreation focuses on fishing in nearby Lake Almanor at the extreme northern end of the Sierra. Vacationers and retirees now bolster an economy once driven by logging.

any month of the year to make hypothermia a constant threat.

Tahoe—or hell for that matter—could freeze over before I could walk out of a casino with pockets heavier than when I entered. But the heady scent of risk and the hope that springs eternal stirred excitement as I waded into the music of clinking coins and ringing slot machines at Stateline, where gambling dens mark where Nevada begins. The same scent of risk draws many visitors to the tables of Tahoe, where annual gaming revenue reaches 350 million dollars. The hotel and gaming industries make up about 40 percent of the area's employment base. Perhaps as a tribute to high times and transient glory, this casino sported a decor of ancient Rome, with fluted faux columns and lovely women in mini-togas serving free drinks.

I wandered the floor, observing mounds of chips move back and forth across the craps table and following the ball in the roulette wheel. I finally settled in a blackjack chair next to a woman whose pile of chips I roughly estimated at $1,700. Her bets ran in the hundreds, mine in single digits. In a while her husband appeared at her side, suggesting they move on. She placed one more bet of $500, lost it, and left seemingly unfazed.

I left too, after my self-imposed loss limit had been reached, and bought ten dollars worth of quarters to feed a slot machine. *Clang, clang, clang* went my occasional winnings in the tray below, and I devised an experiment. I would feed all quarters into the machine, then feed my winnings through as well, as long as they lasted. Ten dollars became $6.20, which became $3.80, which became nothing, except for three quarters I stuck in my pocket for parking meters. A fairly predictable rate of loss, unless I hit a jackpot.

On the way out I passed the mother of all slots, an eight-foot machine with an arm that required both hands to pull it and a sign that promised the chance to win a million dollars. Knowing the odds, I never gave it a second look. The next day I read in the local paper that Emerita Nagal, a Philippine immigrant, had put three quarters in such a machine the previous night and won $1,231,002.

More than money brings permanent residents to the area. Joe Rubini and Lucy Woolshlager live and work in the San Francisco Bay area but hope to move permanently to their cabin at the edge of Desolation Wilderness above Tahoe. "We love cold weather," said Lucy, as their seven-month-old daughter Sophia chortled and threw spoons on the floor as fast as her parents could replace them. "We love to snowshoe and ski and we love the woods. The bears come down at night and raid our trash cans," she added pridefully.

Not everyone reacts so positively to the confrontation with wildlife as the suburbs spread into the woods. Complaints pour in to the California Department of Fish and Game of deer eating shrubs, bears tipping garbage cans, and cougars snatching pets.

"Normally, deer come from high elevations down to 1,000 to 4,000 feet in winter to forage," said Ron Bertram, Fish and Game biologist for

Region Two at the north end of the range. "Forty percent of the deer's winter range in Butte County has been subdivided, although maybe not built on yet. With people irrigating lawns and planting shrubs, deer stop migrating and hang out on golf courses and in backyards. Local deer in and around subdivisions may increase because of the availability of irrigated and fertilized forage throughout the year. They become tame and lose their fear of people. In fall, the bucks go into rut and may attack people. Tame deer quit following their usual patterns and eventually may die from malnutrition or disease. Their reproductive success is poor."

Cougars, or mountain lions, follow the deer, but they may also take alternatives. "They love pets—dogs and cats," said Bertram, "Sometimes they come in confrontation with people and may take them as prey."

As the numbers of protected cougars increase, Fish and Game has issued advisories on avoiding attacks: Do not run. Stay upright. Maintain eye contact. Fight back with sticks and stones. Throughout the range, park notices recommend against hiking, and especially jogging, alone. In 1994 jogger Barbara Schoener, mother of two children, was hit from behind and killed by a female cougar seeking nourishment to nurse her cub.

Cougars usually leave people alone, according to Becky Pierce, who studied the big cats over a six-year period for a doctoral thesis. "They could attack people every day if they wanted to," she said as we bounced in a pickup over subdivided rangeland. "I have watched lions sleeping in the brush within 20 feet of a trail where people were walking by regularly and never knew a lion was there. But they are very opportunistic, and if a mountain lion is hungry and sees a person alone, especially if the person is running, the mountain lion may see the runner as prey."

Driving the pickup was Vernon Bleich of Fish and Game, who wanted to look at a piece of prime wintering ground for mule deer that was about to sprout with houses. "The development couldn't be in a worse place," he said. "Those houses will be smack in the middle of a route the deer use to move to high country in spring and back down in winter."

That was in February. No deer had yet moved to the highlands by May 28 when Carolyn Tiernan, an emergency room physician in Bishop, took me cross-country skiing over Tioga Pass. Snowplows had cleared Route 120 to a point near the crest. Beyond the barricades, drifts all but covered the park rangers' buildings that mark the eastern entrance to Yosemite National Park.

We skied into the park's Dana Meadows in bright sunshine. Vast fields of white stretched before us, dotted with lodgepole pine, their branches drooping with snow. World-class in master's competitive cross-country, Carolyn literally skied rings around me, zigzagging at high speed to maintain her conditioning while my flatlander lungs gasped for oxygen at nearly 10,000 feet. We tramped down a spot with our skis near a stand of pines and sat down for lunch, relishing an unspoiled view. "This is the best time

Wind and water bring
sailboats out on Lake
Tahoe for weekly races in
spring and summer. A
magnet for sailors, the
high, blue waters trapped
by geologic uplift have
attracted admirers for
more than a century,
but two attempts to create
a national park have
failed. Longtime residents
laud Tahoe's charms but
lament the relentless foul-
ing of its waters. Silt from
development has dulled
the lake's long-famous
clarity in some places.

to see the meadows," she said. "When the snow melts, the visitors start pouring through."

That snow means later fun for the millions who enjoy water sports. At the extreme southern end of the Sierra, snow was long gone from the lowlands, but melt from the high country had the Kern River cold and raging. My wife, Barbara, joined me for a white-water raft trip down the Kern, and we squeezed into waist-high wet suits to ward off the chill of icy splashes, which, we were guaranteed, would be forthcoming.

"Because of the large amount of snowfall this winter, the river is running about twice its average flow," said Matt Schreiber, the guide in our rubber raft, "which makes for exciting rafting."

The rolling, dusty hills northeast of Bakersfield have not escaped the exodus of urbanites. Vacation and retirement homes now ring Isabella Lake, formed by damming the Kern in 1952. Crowds of people come to run the river in spring and summer both above and below the dam. "When my wife and I retired here 20 years ago, people just came and rafted the river by themselves, for fun," said Wayne Requa of Kernville. Now four rafting companies carry clients through maelstroms of leaping foam.

We boarded our raft below Isabella Lake along with two law students from Los Angeles, Kristi Gasaway and Mia Noble. River guide Matt sat in back to direct our paddling so we would avoid capsizing or being folded over a boulder. Mia, the only one with no white-water experience, looked concerned but game. We paddled into a current that shot us downriver like a leaf in a street gutter.

The names of the rapids—Hari-kari, Surprise, Pinball, Eat Rocks and Bleed—hardly engender confidence in the novice. Most difficult would be the one called Horseshoe, which sounded harmless until Matt explained, "That's the shape your raft assumes if you don't go through it right."

The canyon, lined with oaks and grasslands, soon rang with jubilant cries as we charged through thundering waters, Matt shouting paddling instructions from the rear, *"Forward three, right turn...all forward!"* Splashes of cold spray were forgotten in rushes of adrenaline. Mia's expression changed from concern to elation.

We went into Horseshoe Falls facing a backwave that rose higher than our heads after the river poured over a steep drop-off. *"All forward!"* yelled Matt, and five paddles dug into the foam. Horseshoe didn't bend us, but it spat us off to the side and among the hanging branches of a willow at streamside. Untangling ourselves, we eased back into the current and went through two more rapids before pulling for the bank at our take-out point.

"What a great break from the law books!" exclaimed Kristi, beaming.

Mia, now a white-water veteran, already looked forward to future weekends. "Do you have any ideas for other fun things we can do like this?"

The Sierra had just won two more enthusiasts. ∎

FOLLOWING PAGES:
Above the clouds, Diamond Peak at 8,540 feet receives the morning sun. More than 30 miles of ski trails lace its southern face, the longest a continuous drop of two and a half miles and 1,840 feet in altitude. More than a dozen ski resorts in the Tahoe area, blanketed by some of the world's highest annual snowfalls, play host to millions annually. A boon to thrill seekers today, the steep slopes and deep snows long blocked settlement of the California coast by European immigrants from the east. Now the verticality and generous moisture bolster the Sierran economy, as vacationers delight in winter and water sports.

Snowfall veils conifers near Spooner Lake on the Nevada side of Lake Tahoe. In search of game, Native Americans ascended to the cool heights of the Sierra in summer but retreated to the oak foothills when frost rimed the needles (left).

FOLLOWING PAGES:
A pristine world of silence surrounds a skiing trekker pulling a sled of provisions over frozen Lower Echo Lake south of Tahoe. Heavy recreational use of the Sierra can crowd pop-ular trails in summer. Traversing the same ground, winter users can still find solitude amid splendid scenery.

With conveniences that early pioneers could not have imagined, camper Tom Hafner prepares an evening repast as his canine companion stands nearby. A headlamp spotlights dinner as it warms over a propane stove. Light from a gas lantern reflects from cross-country skis propped in the drifts. Fighting their way through deep Sierra snows in the winter of 1843-44, a party led by explorer John C. Frémont swathed their faces in black silk to prevent snow blindness. In the cold and misery they lost 71 horses and mules; one man was driven mad.

Spring lends a blush to a hillside near Kernville, as wildflowers bloom in the southern Sierra. Both moisture and mountain height tail off at the extreme southern end of the range, entry point for fur trapper Jed Smith, who wandered into Spanish California in 1826. Ordered out by the governor, he drifted north and in 1827 made the first recorded winter crossing back to the east, with great difficulty. By mid-year, flowers and grasses wither in the south, but ample rains in the north nurture forests and vegetation such as these broad-leafed corn lilies (top, right) in Plumas National Forest near Quincy, California. Rain-soaked moss in the Plumas provides a playground for a rough-skinned newt (bottom, right).

FOLLOWING PAGES:
Rocks wear shrouds of moss nourished by frequent winter rains in Plumas National Forest. Beyond the oak trees courses the Middle Fork of the Feather River, one of nine national wild, scenic, and recreational rivers in the Sierra.

PRECEDING PAGES:
Moonrise captivates a hiker near Carson Pass, named for mountain man Kit Carson who joined John C. Frémont on expeditions over the Sierra. Strong and steady winds blasting high bluffs at 9,000 feet have forced a conifer to branch only on the leeward side. Wind also buffets hikers on the Pacific Crest Trail, who are rewarded with breathtaking views. Nearly 1,000 of its 2,400 miles stretching from Canada to Mexico ribbon the ridges of the Sierra.

Angry water challenges rafters in the Merced River. A quiet stream through much of Yosemite National Park, the Merced becomes a torrent as it heads past Arch Rock Entrance near the town of El Portal. The Tuolumne River, tamed at its headwaters in the park, cuts a gash through Stanislaus National Forest (opposite). In 1894, a plan to dam the Tuolumne River and flood the Hetch Hetchy Valley led naturalist John Muir to rage, "Dam Hetch Hetchy! As well dam for water-tanks the people's cathedrals and churches...."

Rushing to join Lake
Tahoe, frothing waters
dance down Eagle Falls
above the early morning
stillness of Emerald Bay.
For all the gold and tim-
ber taken from the moun-
tain range, water remains
the most important
resource of the Sierra
Nevada. Boon to recre-
ationists, bounty for valley
garden crops, and a gift of
life for millions in arid
cities along the coast,
water is at the heart of
environmental concerns
about human impact on
the mountain slopes. For-
est removal, road-build-
ing, and subdivisions sully
the streams that supply
nearly half the runoff in
all of California.

JEWELS OF THE

SIERRA

"MOUNT WHITNEY IN SUMMER," SNIFFED ONE SIERRA PURIST concerned about excessive visitation, "looks like one of those Dr. Seuss books with a string of people connected to the top of a mountain."

To many who love both the Sierra and solitude, it may seem like a crowd, but between May 22 and October 15, in fact, 200 people a day receive climbing permits to the highest point in the lower 48 states. So massive is the mountain that someone gazing on it from below would be unlikely to see anyone scaling the sheer eastern wall, let alone hiking up the trail. The trail becomes even less crowded off season because climbers have to contend with snow and cold. Still, some 30,000 ascend annually to Mount Whitney's flat-topped peak at 14,494 feet, and thousands more tip back their heads on a clear day to admire it from the base, paying homage to one of the jewels in a range loaded with ornaments.

The Sierra could be called an embarrassment of riches. Ten percent of its entire 15.5 million acres has been declared national parkland, and 60 percent of the remainder enjoys some sort of protection under federal or state governments. While urban immigrants and visitors spread out over the range for the sights and recreation, a few gems stand out as the main draws: Mount Whitney, Yosemite Valley, the giant sequoias, and Kings Canyon.

Of these Mount Whitney receives the fewest on-site visitors because of the limited facilities on the route to the top. For those who prefer to admire rather than ascend, a short drive on Portal Road west of the town of Lone Pine offers a full view of the mountain. For extreme contrasts, you can drive in just a few hours from Death Valley, California, the lowest point in North America, to the base of Whitney, from which you can hike up to the highest point in the lower 48 states. The two lie fewer than 80 air miles apart.

Although the east side looks sheer and formidable, it presents a walkable incline. The 22-mile climb from the car park to the top and back can be made in one day by the super fit. Most hikers choose to camp partway up and ascend the mountain in two days, as the sudden 6,000-foot change in altitude can cause dizziness and nausea.

Eying the high road ahead, two hikers contemplate their route up Mount Whitney just before breaking camp for their second day of climbing. Beyond them towers the crest of the Sierra, of which Whitney is the highest point. In summer the well-marked route to the top requires no technical climbing gear. Octogenarians have completed the 22-mile round-trip—some in a single day.

From the summit, a cavalcade of peaks marches off to the north, more than a dozen of them over 13,000 feet. Mount Williamson, some six miles north, just misses Whitney's height at 14,375, and Mount Tyndall next to it tops 14,000. To the east across five-mile-wide Owens Valley, the White Mountains present peaks of almost equal height. Despite their name, they get less snow than the Sierra, which steals moisture from the clouds before they cross the valley. Mountains exceeding 14,000 feet on either side make Owens the deepest valley in North America.

Not the deepest, but perhaps the most scenic valley in the world lies 110 miles northwest of Whitney in Yosemite National Park. More than four million people arrive every year to see a host of geologic wonders clustered in a seven-by-one-mile declivity—Yosemite Valley.

"There they are, just to the left of the little hump," I heard someone say as I walked a footpath in Yosemite and approached a group with three pairs of binoculars pointed upward. I followed the slant of the glasses and stared hard at the smooth, gleaming face of El Capitan, but could see nothing. "Climbers," said one of the watchers, and handed me his glasses. I picked out three antlike figures clinging the monolith. Despite having some experience at rock climbing, the sight of the three on the 3,500-foot sheer wall set my stomach fluttering.

Most of the awe-inspiring sights in Yosemite Valley can only be taken in at a distance. North Dome presents a huge, rounded cathedral-like top at the east end of the valley, and perhaps Half Dome across from it would have also, had not frost and glaciers smoothly sheared one side. Yosemite Falls rushes down 1,430 feet in its first unobstructed leap, then surges through cascades before free-falling another 320 feet, for a total drop of nearly half a mile. Across the valley, Bridalveil Fall pours over a lower cliff in a wide plume of white that inspired its romantic name. Other works of nature also inspire lengthy contemplation: Cathedral Rocks, Glacier Point, Cathedral Spire, Sentinel Dome, the Royal Arches, Mirror Lake, the Merced River.

Surrounding these treasures, Yosemite National Park totals 1,169 square miles, about the size of Rhode Island. Nearly 200 miles of paved roads carry visitors to scenery also spectacular and far more serene. Tioga Road, when finally cleared of snow in June or July, leads to the high country, past lovely Tenaya Lake, mirroring huge slabs of granite, and through the sunny, verdant Tuolumne Meadows. Hetch Hetchy Road leads to the Hetch Hetchy Valley, dammed in 1923 to create a reservoir. The Tuolumne River is still popular with kayakers, who test their skills farther downriver.

Glacier Point Road leads to a view of Yosemite Valley from atop cliffs 3,200 feet high. Wawona Road dips into the south end of the park and into Mariposa Grove, one of three small stands of giant sequoias in the park.

In addition to the paved roads, 67 miles of graded roads pass by quiet lakes, sunny meadows, and pillars of rock. The more intimate look may be afoot or on horseback, for 840 miles of trails weave through the park.

But Yosemite Valley remains the star attraction, a place where the flow of water and ice have created some of nature's finest artistry. The Merced River first carved a deep valley after a huge mass of granite rose out of inner Earth. The dip became a chute for massive glaciers that widened the valley even more and scoured the sheer cliff faces.

Rivers poured off the high cliffs to plummet in waves of mist before flowing quietly through the valley. Where the glacier stopped and eventually melted, rocks piled up in a terminal moraine, forming a dam at the valley's western end and creating wet meadows that left much of the valley open.

The first to enjoy these spectacular sights were Native Americans known as the Miwok. They occupied the valley for nearly 4,000 years, subsisting on acorns, berries, and bulbs, hunting deer with bows and arrows, and trapping squirrels and birds with snares of woven grass. Acorns made up perhaps half their diet. Peeled and pounded, rinsed with water to leach tannic acid, then boiled, they provided a mush with 6 percent protein and considerable potassium, said to be good for the nerves.

"It must be good for you," chirped 70-year-old Julia Parker, who grew up as a coastal Pomo Indian and married into the Yosemite Miwok lineage. "My husband's great-grandmother lived to be 112."

Well versed in Miwok lore, Julia demonstrates their skills at the Indian Cultural Museum at Yosemite National Park headquarters in the valley. "Indian ways were disappearing because of the influence of non-Indian people," she told me, "but my husband's family thought the old ways were important and should be preserved."

As we talked, she demonstrated a time-honored skill, plucking root hairs from a tuber she called a "soap root" to make a brush. She bunched them, then soaked one end with juice from the plant. The juice hardened into a cement, holding the hairs together and forming a handle. "They used brushes of soap root to sweep off a work place or to clean out a woven basket. There were small ones used only to brush their hair." She led me outside to a wooded area to show how the Miwok dug up soap root with a sharp stick.

"People who were raised by their grandparents used to share all they knew," she said. "The old ones had the wisdom, the young ones were the vessel to receive it, and those in the middle years demonstrated what they had learned. The three levels don't work that way anymore. There was no squabbling among families then."

"They were not a warlike people," agreed Bob Fry, a non-Indian student of Miwok culture for some 30 years who has earned respect among surviving Miwok as a maker of primitive tools and weapons. A few feet from where Julia fashioned brushes, he knapped razor-sharp arrowheads from obsidian and twisted the outer covering of dogbane into a stout string. "As long as there was proper respect, outside groups would be tolerated," he said.

They must have guarded their territory vigorously, for the valley's name stems from a word used to describe them by outside Miwok. They called the valley residents *yohemite,* which translates into "some of them are killers."

The real killers were whites who came looking for gold. Beginning in 1851, an invading militia called the Mariposa Battalion killed Miwok who resisted and twice tried—unsuccessfully—to relocate them. As more whites settled in and around the valley, Miwok numbers shrank. Those who survived disease and violence adopted Euro-American dress and worked for their new neighbors.

To preserve the valley's beauty, President Abraham Lincoln signed a grant entrusting the area to California in 1864. The budding park service blasted holes in the glacial moraine in the late 1800s to release water and dry up some of the wet meadows to accommodate visitors. Without the meadows, conifers grew. Photographs from 1866, 1941, 1966, and 1998 show progressively more vegetation on the valley floor, which had about 50 percent more open space in 1866 than it does now. In the words of one of today's Miwok: "The white man came to Yosemite and turned it into a wilderness."

It was hardly an empty wilderness. Roads ringed the valley to accommodate automobiles. Campfires polluted the evening air with a smoky haze. Hotels, gift shops, restaurants, and residences for park employees sprouted among the trees.

I drove to Yosemite Valley in winter, when snow on either side of the road in the surrounding mountains rose higher than my car and clumps of it cascaded off conifer branches in long, white plumes. On the quiet valley floor I generally walked alone on the paths in crisp, clean air, and stood at the base of Lower Yosemite Fall hearing nothing but the hiss of water on stone. Yosemite Village near park headquarters had the activity level of a small town.

I returned Memorial Day weekend to hordes of people, honking horns, the growl of tour buses, and the smell of exhaust fumes. Twice I tried to revisit Lower Yosemite Fall, but could not find a parking place. El Capitan still dazzled with the play of light against its smooth face; green meadows and wildflowers made a colorful foreground for Cathedral Rocks, but the small town had become a metropolis.

With fewer trees, the Miwok had better views, and quieter ones.

To return a more natural look to this stunning geological setting and offer tourists a quieter, cleaner, and less congested visit, the National Park Service began discussing changes in 1974, but nothing happened. Nature sped up the work with a huge flood of the Merced River in 1997 that tore away buildings and cut through roads. Since the new plan called for removal of some of the facilities, it made no sense to restore them all. The park is in the process of rebuilding out of the floodplain.

In the new Yosemite Valley, visitors may drive to the park but will leave their cars in remote parking lots and travel through the valley in electric shuttle buses, getting off at points to hike on their own. Familiar roads and bridges will disappear; bicycle and pedestrian trails will increase. Campgrounds will be moved to less conspicuous areas. Some trees will be removed, and meadows will be restored to open up the valley again to a broader view.

"These have been sticky issues," said park ranger Jerry Mitchell, the man in charge of shepherding the Valley Implementation Plan. "Some people with fond memories of camping here didn't want familiar campgrounds wiped out, or they were attached to the attractive stone bridges built by the Works Progress Administration in the thirties and didn't want to see them go. Some businessmen near the park said that reduction of cars would adversely affect their businesses. But we have to look at the larger question—how to retain the charm of the valley and make it enjoyable for people even in congested summer months. Services, accommodations, and campgrounds will be here, but relocated."

"We want the valley to be dominated by its character, not by the automobile," he continues. "There should be sounds of the river, the birds, and the waterfalls, not sounds of diesel buses."

Loyalties to this much loved valley run high. I joined a tour designed to introduce the proposed changes in late January 1998. Of the handful of people that boarded the bus, one woman had journeyed from the Los Angeles area to hear the explanations from park rangers and to register her complaints.

"I've heard what they have in mind for this place," she said indignantly, "and I just want to see for myself if there is any more logic than I can discern. If they think they are going to tear down Stoneman BRIDGE, I'm going to be standing in front of it," and she spread her arms wide as if to guard against such an atrocity. "They say it interrupts the flow of the river. Well, change the construction of the bridge!" Her eyes tilted skyward in exasperation.

"Hydrologists and biologists are looking at these things, determining what is best for the park," Jerry Mitchell told me. "We'll make changes as the money is available," said Jerry, "but I think if you return in 2005 you'll see quite a different park, more natural and less dominated by the automobile and traffic congestion."

A hundred miles to the south, Sequoia National Park also stands in danger of being loved to death. At risk are the very attractions that bring visitors, the giant sequoias, largest trees in the world.

Sequoias may tower nearly 300 feet in height, with trunks as large as 30 feet thick including an 18-inch layer of bark. One tree called the Boole in Sequoia National Forest measures 112 feet around. A single limb on the General Sherman tree is 140 feet long and 6.8 feet in diameter. A fast early growth rate allows sequoias to reach considerable size before fire can destroy them. Resistance to insects and disease that would kill other trees has let some reach ages exceeding 3,000 years.

You have to stand next to these behemoths to comprehend their immensity. No photograph does them justice. A heavy fog filled me with disappointment after I drove up the twisting road into the park in late May and stood before the General Sherman, considered the largest of the largest living trees. Its width of 32 feet would completely fill most city streets. As its crown disappeared into grayness, my wife, Barbara, took the romantic view: "Fog only adds to the mystery of how any living thing could be so huge."

For decades, an even greater mystery has been the seeming limits of the sequoias' range. Although related to the coastal redwoods, they live and reproduce only in a 250-mile strip on the western slope of the Sierra Nevada, which seems to provide the right combination of sunlight, cool temperatures, adequate moisture, and deep, but well-drained soils. A third of them grow within Sequoia and Kings Canyon National Parks, and most of the other two-thirds are in Sequoia National Forest. The rest are on public or private land. "You can grow them elsewhere, but generally, they won't reproduce," says Nate Stephenson, a biologist studying the relationship between sequoias and fire.

That relationship couldn't be more intimate. Fire has been the constant companion of the big trees and is the father of new sequoia life. "They appear to need fire to create openness for sunlight, to bare and sterilize the soil, and to cause the cones to release seeds," said Nate.

"They leave us with a wonderful record of fires through the ages," he added, picking up a cross-section of a sequoia that fell in 1869. Researchers have counted the growth rings back to the center, which shows that the tree sprouted in 12 B.C., at the beginning of the Roman Empire. Small black scars in the rings that follow tell of flames that raged through the forest at successive stages of the tree's growth—A.D. 603, 614, 626, 646, 656—about every ten years. "Probably the time it took for brush and forest debris to build up enough to be ignited again and cleaned out," said Nate.

In the past 20 or 30 centuries, the constant cycle of fire has been interrupted only in the most recent 2. Over the past 150 years, Californians have viewed fire as the enemy and suppressed it before the forest can be purged.

"During that time we have seen a virtual halt in sequoia reproduction, with only a couple of cases of small trees getting started," said Nate. "Sequoia groves make up a small part of the Sierran landscape, so we ought to be able to ensure the future by using prescribed fires. But with so many people living nearby now, we may never be able to recreate the fires that used to burn through the rest of the forest because of the concern over air quality standards. We may need creative solutions to maintain forest health."

Admirers have brought more than fire prevention to endanger the big trees.

"In the early days of the parks, no one could imagine the kind of visitation we have now," said William Tweed, chief interpreter at the park and co-author of a book about its history. "So facilities grew up right next to the trees:

roads, buildings, parking lots. Root systems have been covered up with asphalt or cut during road building and sewer installation. We've even cut down sequoias in the past out of fear they might fall on buildings We had to ask ourselves, what's wrong with this picture—cutting down a tree thousands of years old to save a building that could be located elsewhere in months."

Corrections are under way. The 283 guest rooms on park grounds will all be removed by summer 1999. Parking lots will be torn up, more buildings razed, and as in Yosemite, visitors will park some distance from the trees and either walk or travel by shuttle bus to see them. Restaurants, hotels, and gift shops near the trees will be relocated.

Unlike Yosemite, the changes under way at Sequoia National Park meet no public outcry. "People accept the necessity of keeping the prime attraction alive here," said Tweed. "In Yosemite you can tear up roads or put in a parking lot and the falls will still flow, El Capitan will still be there. There's some sadness here at removing old facilities, but people know you can't have a city and a forest in the same location. We're trying to return the Giant Forest to its natural state so it will be here for a long time."

Even the age of the sequoias represents an eye wink in time compared to construction of another extravaganza a few miles away. Heading north from Sequoia National Park, you enter Sequoia National Forest and drive down, down, down through numerous hairpin turns into the gorge cut by the South Fork of the Kings River. Farther upstream in Kings Canyon National Park, the canyon was cut by the river and enlarged by glaciers. But here, the river cut deeper, leaving a V-shaped gash of 8,240 feet, making it one of the deepest canyons in North America.

The instrument for this incision, the Kings River, descends about 12,000 feet over a distance of approximately 100 miles. The river grumbles and roars as it fights past boulders and pours over rock shelves, tossing explosions of spray. Park officials prohibit rafting, which here would be an adventurous form of suicide.

Spanish explorers camping along the river in 1805 named it *el rio de los Santos Reyes*—River of the Holy Kings, for the feast of the Epiphany in the Christian Church when the three kings supposedly arrived with gifts for the Christ child. The name fits. Majesty reigns.

If you prefer your jewels rough cut, visit Kings Canyon. The Park Service has limited road-building to one route that ends at the Cedar Grove campgrounds and lodge. Beyond lies wilderness and myriad quiet trails.

"The decision was made in the 1950s to keep it a wilderness park," says park interpreter William Tweed. "Still, about 600,000 people a year come for a visit."

Like many other visitors, I armed myself with a trail map, parked my car at road's end, and set off near the South Fork of the Kings. House-size rocks lay by the trail, and one could only imagine the commotion raised when

With an artist's hand, Elizabeth Sutton captures the dramatic effect of morning light on the sheer face of Half Dome. She and half a dozen other painters share a meadow in Yosemite Valley to render their own interpretations of the 4,733-foot mound of cracked granite.

Sketches by artist Thomas Ayres and others in the mid-1800s helped introduce the wonders of Yosemite to the world. Ayres's paintings inspired tourists to endure two-day stage rides from the nearest train station and helped spur Congress to protect the scenic area.

they broke loose from the cliffs above to tumble into the gorge hundreds, maybe thousands of years before. Two browsing deer merely moved aside as I passed, as if I had entered some kind of peaceable kingdom.

Heaven, however, lay six miles and 1,500 vertical feet ahead. My destination was Paradise Valley, a high, wide opening in the Kings River Canyon that John Muir in his usual passion for the moment once said rivaled Yosemite. Springy pine needles and fine sand on level ground gave way to granite and heart-thumping steepness. The trail moved to riverside where the river spoke in royal, sonorous tones.

At 5,663 feet I passed Mist Falls, where a brief but brutal drop in the river pounds water into tiny, airborne droplets. A few hundred feet above the falls I encountered a crew of young workers with the California Conservation Corps, moving boulders on a sun-blasted granite slope to create steps marking the pathway. Her sweat-streaked face beaming with happiness, 20-year-old Shawna Merrick-Lemos explained why she took the five-month job at minimum wage: "It's awesome country. I love working out here."

The trail grew steeper but had its rewards: Each view back down the canyon was more spectacular than the last. Piñon pines, a rare feature on the west side of the Sierra, grew in twisted profile against the canyon walls.

I knew I'd reached Paradise by the silence and the end of my labors. The trail suddenly leveled out, and the river ran silent and smooth as glass. I strode through tall columns of pines that opened onto a grassy meadow, where the water made a lazy bend and curled back on itself in a deep pool. My back against a boulder, I ate lunch and watched a small trout wander lazily beneath a half-submerged log. Few of the rock formations around me matched the combined wonders of El Capitan, Half Dome, or Sentinel Rock, and I concluded that what really captivated Muir had been the serenity of solitude amid natural beauty.

After exploring perhaps half of the four-mile-long valley and admiring the cliffs on either side, I reluctantly started back down. I had shared this place with no one that I could see. I hoped the same for hikers I met on my descent, for several bore tents and sleeping bags for an overnight stay. Solitude must have been anticipated by one young woman I met, who was backpacking topless.

"Hello," she said cheerily, as if her dis-attire were the most natural thing in the world, which of course it was.

"Hi," I responded, carefully studying the trail before me.

For millions, the Sierra Nevada range offers the chance to view geologic sights so extraordinary they have become national icons. For a young woman en route to Paradise, and for the many hikers who choose roads less traveled, the Sierra offers the chance to step joyously back into a simpler and more basic existence. ■

Amid a palette of fall color, a buck mule deer, well-equipped with antlers for rut season battles, samples a leaf of milkweed. A pod of the plant, named for its white sap, offers its seeds to the wind (above). Deer, black bear, and coyotes wander the valley seemingly oblivious to the constant human presence. Bears made fearless by unarmed visitors pose a problem, sometimes smashing into locked cars if they smell anything edible inside.

Learning age-old skills from the hands of her elders, young Naomi Jones gathers bunchgrass for weaving baskets. Her Miwok ancestors collected the material along the Merced River (top left), where fall frosts turn its color to buff. The hands of her great-grandmother Julia Parker shape a new basket (below, left) at the Indian Cultural Museum in Yosemite Valley, where she shares Indian lore with visitors. Invasion by gold-seeking whites sparked skirmishes with the Miwok, who resisted signing a treaty with the newcomers. Rooted out by a state-sponsored volunteer militia known as the Mariposa Battalion, the Indians returned as park employees but gradually blended into the white culture of California. Called "Yohemite" by other tribes, the group gave the valley its name.

FOLLOWING PAGES: A vertical river thunders before two who walked a challenging mile and a half out of Yosemite Valley to view Vernal Fall. The path to the top earned the name Mist Trail because water atomized on the rocks drifts over it in a coat-soaking fog.

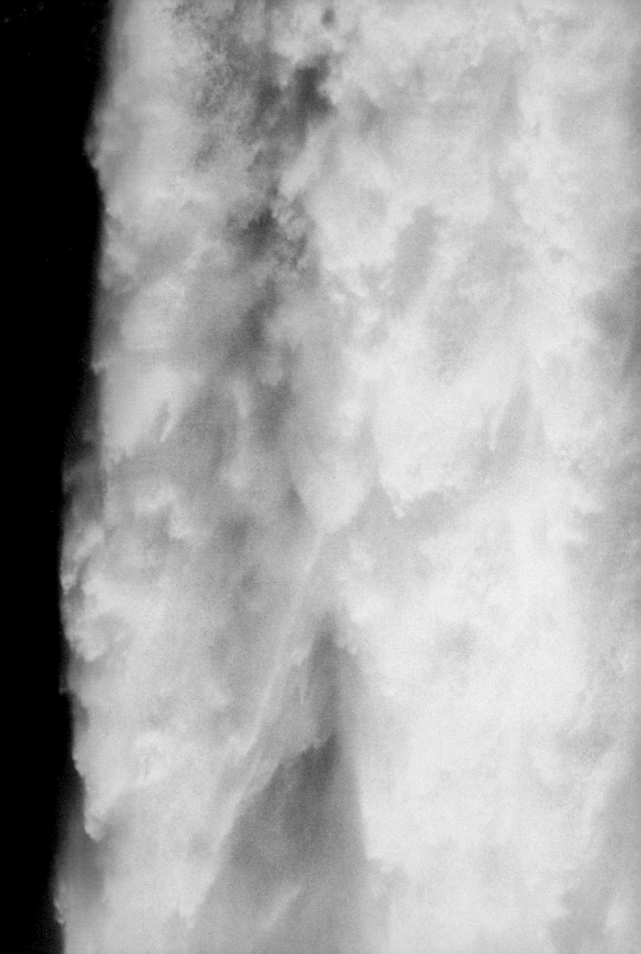

At home in the heights, rock climber Mike Corbett leans back to survey the route ahead on the face of El Capitan. Veteran of some 50 ascents, Corbett, like many others, sleeps overnight during the assault in a sling dangling above the valley floor.

Sunset cannot dignify a forest scorched and blackened by a fire in western Yosemite Park in 1990. The squelching of natural fires started by lightning over the past century may have added to the destruction. Park officials say the buildup of brushy fuel now results in huge conflagrations that alter the growth that would normally follow. Purposely set and controlled burns bring public complaints of reduced air quality. Showing promise of rebirth after a fire, young ponderosa pines spring up on the forest floor (above, right). Signaling spring, snow plants push through pine needles as soon as melt finally bares the ground. Their bright color results from a lack of chlorophyll.

Echoing exploration of the Sierra in the 19th century, horsepackers at 7,000 feet follow the Copper Creek Trail in Kings Canyon National Park, jointly administered with adjacent Sequoia National Park. The two form a superpark 66 miles long and 36 miles wide, where a trekker can be farther from a road than anywhere else in the lower 48 states. This group left the Cedar Grove Pack Station bound for Granite Basin through a region deliberately left wild, a decision made in the 1950s. Only one road spears into the park, winding down Kings Canyon and ending at Cedar Grove. "Research has shown that a road can disturb wildlife for three miles on either side of it," said a park ranger and interpreter.

The South Fork of the
Kings River rushes down-
slope at speeds that helped
cut one of the deepest
canyons in North Amer-
ica. The highest wall rises
more than a mile and a
half above the rock-gnaw-
ing waters. Carrying
snowmelt down from lakes
at 12,000 feet, the river
reaches sea level within a
hundred miles. The pre-
cipitous drop rules out
white-water sports, but
backpackers rejoice in
hundreds of square miles
of wilderness. Blossoms of
a California buckeye
bring a softness to steep,
rugged slopes (right).

FOLLOWING PAGES:
Doubling the pleasure of
Kearsarge Pinnacles in
Kings Canyon National
Park, glassy Kearsarge
Lake presents a mirror
image. At an elevation of
11,500 feet, only the
sturdy-legged and stout-
lunged can enjoy the view.

PRECEDING PAGES:
Wresting a living in high country, a Jeffrey pine sends gnarled roots over rocks near Eagle Lake. Roots that probe deep into cracks at high altitude allow the hardy Jeffrey, named for its Scottish discoverer, to survive for five centuries in soils that would daunt other pines.

Twilight darkens Jeffrey pines while setting distant Mineral and Sawtooth Peaks aglow in Sequoia National Park. The gradual ascent to this popular lookout near Eagle Lake appeals to beginning hikers. Most visitors to Sequoia drive to within feet of the park's main attraction at lower altitudes. Park plans call for mass transit to the sequoias to reduce damage to them from the compacting of surrounding soils.

The view from Moro Rock at sunset captivates a mother and her towhead. Auto road and hiking trail lead to lookouts on the granite monolith, one of a number of dome formations in the Sierra. Pressure deep within the Earth forced molten rock upward, which cooled to become granite. As erosion gradually stripped away the heavy overburden from large blocks, the granite expanded, flaking off material along curved fracture lines and creating round-topped mountains like Moro (opposite).

Nature in the raw: a visitor to Moro Rock finds a secluded place to shed his clothes and meditate in celebration of summer solstice. Despite heavy visitation to star attractions within the Sierra Nevada's three national parks—Sequoia, Kings Canyon, and Yosemite—vast areas remain where lovers of the outdoors can find solitude. More than a million people annually visit adjoining Sequoia and Kings Canyon, most of them adhering to main roads and the giant trees, while perhaps 30,000 wander through backcountry larger in area than Rhode Island. Fewer than 400 enjoy the silence and uncluttered scenery of the High Sierra Trail, an eight-day, 70-mile hike to the east and the top of Mount Whitney.

THE EASTERN ES

CARPMENT

The Eastern Escarpment

Most people hope they never encounter a cougar, or mountain lion, as Californians call them, in the wild. John Wehausen tracks them on the steep, rocky slopes along the eastern side of the Sierra, study-ing their habits, fretting about their latest meal. A wildlife biologist, his chief concern lies not with the sleek, tawny lions but the bighorn sheep that share their habitat in the heights above Owens Valley.

"Recent research on their DNA and skull shape has found that these sheep are a separate subspecies related to but distinguishable from the desert bighorn sheep of the Southwest," he told me as we drove in his pickup south along the valley floor. "Now there may be no more than 120 individuals left, and the lions seek them as prey. I've found 49 lion-killed sheep carcasses in just one population, and, of course, I didn't find them all."

To the west, the eastern front of the Sierra Nevada soars to 14,000 feet from the desert floor. To the east and across the valley, the White Moun-tains loom nearly as high. If you live in Owens Valley, you may have a spec-tacular view from any window in your house.

"Mountain lions were once threatened by hunting," said John, "but public sentiment shifted in their favor, and various legislative acts have pro-tected them since the early seventies. With high deer densities for food, lion numbers increased steadily. By the mid-eighties, the lion population in this area had a devastating effect on Sierra bighorn, and deer populations declined precipitously at the same time."

Working with grant money to study the sheep–lion relationship, John harbors no anger toward the big cats. "I'm not anti-lion," he said. "I want everything to be here. But if one native species is driving another to extinc-tion due to past human intrusion, I think we have an obligation to take action to assure continuance of both."

He has witnessed the power and skills of the cougar at close range. Once, while creeping near a cougar feeding on a deer kill so he could shoot it with a tranquilizer gun and place a radio collar around its neck, the animal charged. "It came right over a bunch of willows that were eight feet high,"

A bleak existence both inside and out of slab-sided housing faced miners at Bodie, a gold-fed outpost in the eastern Sierra. Rich veins underground brought a mini-rush after the placer gold in streams on the western slope had been picked over. The Rev. F. M. Warrington described the town in 1881 as "a sea of sin, lashed by the tempests of lust and passion." Fire leveled much of the town in 1932, and when the only school was closed eight years later, Bodie was virtually abandoned. The town became a state historic park in 1962.

he remembers. "I backpedaled about ten yards, and it finally stopped and went back to eating."

He also saw a cougar snatch a full-grown 130-pound sheep from a rocky promontory and bring it to lower ground the same way a cat would carry a mouse. Concern that this might happen again has driven him to the mountains on this day, armed with a receiver that takes signals from a collared lion he calls "Number 780."

We left John's pickup and started up the slope above the canyon, the receiver emitting faint *thump-thumps* that indicated the lion lurked somewhere nearby. On we crunched over snow and through sage and bitterbrush that provide winter sheep forage. John's voice grew softer as the signal grew stronger, until its loud *thump-thumps* played a duet with my own heart.

"Damn," he whispered, "he's right up that draw where the sheep are. I'll bet he's over a kill." He studied the ground below us, with its tangle of willows and labyrinth of ravines. "Finding him can take hours, and I don't have time," he said, finally. "I've got to get back to Bishop for a rehearsal."

My chance to see a cougar in the wild—thwarted by an orchestra concert. Fortunately, I like classical music almost as much as wildlife. The disappointment I felt on the mountainside was erased later by the Eastern Sierra Chamber Orchestra and Chorus, made up of local doctors, construction workers, teachers, retailers, and one bighorn sheep researcher. Hours after tracking lions through sagebrush, John Wehausen played an oboe counterpoint to the clarinet of his wife, Carolyn Tiernan, in a passage from ballet music by Franz Schubert. A 16-year-old high school sophomore named Jane Hatter sang difficult arpeggios from Henry Purcell's opera *Dido and Aeneas*. The role of Dido was performed by Ann Hoffmann, the wife of a national park ranger, who had begun taking voice lessons four months earlier.

"We're about 260 miles from the nearest big city (Los Angeles), so if you want culture in a place like this, you have to make it yourself," said Carolyn Tiernan, physician, competitive cross-country skier, and clarinetist.

When you cross the ridge into the eastern Sierra, you enter a world apart. No clusters of small towns here, primping their old hotels and assay offices to draw weekend tourists. Houses lie widely scattered, and Herefords graze in pastures that look big as counties. Bishop is the cultural center for Inyo County and the hub of an area with a population of about 10,400.

"I love it here because of the wide-open spaces," said Walt Hoffmann, park ranger, snow surveyor, and real-life husband of the neophyte Dido. They live 35 miles north of Bishop in the even smaller town of Benton. "Looking out my window, it's easy to imagine there isn't a barbed wire fence between here and Salt Lake City."

The entire eastern front of the Sierra Nevada can be viewed from Highway 395, which threads the valley just to the east of the range. You begin at Ridgecrest in the far south, where the desert air surrounds your car like a hot blanket, and head north to where the Inyo and White Mountains challenge Whitney across the valley. On through Bishop and past Mammoth Lakes, which you can't see, and Mono Lake, which you can, recovering after a dramatic rescue from overuse. You pass through Carson City, Nevada's capital, and past Reno's casinos if you're able to resist, then make a long, lonely drive through grassy hills to Susanville at the north end of the range.

And always at your left window looms the eastern edge of the Sierra Nevada, sometimes leaping so abruptly out of the desert that it seems a quick left-hand turn might set your car on its rear bumper. Dazzling though it may be, you can enjoy most of the range with the solitude of a first discoverer.

The gold that peopled the western slopes failed to crowd the eastern edge of the range. The best of the placer gold that drew forty-niners to Coloma, Placerville, and Sutter Creek had nearly played out when Waterman S. Body found color in the eastern highlands in 1859, east of today's Yosemite National Park. Gold fever struck anew, and the town of Bodie sprang up, the spelling of its name altered to avoid mispronunciation.

By 1879 Bodie had a population of about 10,000, but municipal success was never in the cards for the damp, chilly location. Snow lingers until June, and spring melt reveals only rock, dust, and scattered vegetation. Bodie's boisterous residents apparently took little cheer from the climate and their own prospects, for the town was said to be second to none in wickedness and violence. There were 65 saloons. Bells tolled the ages of those killed in fights and robberies, and they rang often. Little wonder that a young girl penned in her diary before moving there with her parents, "Good-bye God, I'm going to Bodie."

While the boom lasted into the 1880s, some 30 companies took out 90 to 100 million dollars in gold bullion. The town might have continued on its own inertia, but on July 25, 1892, a fire wiped out all but a few buildings. Some rebuilding was done, but fire struck again in 1932, and with the source of its economy depleted, Bodie staggered into the 1940s with a skeleton citizenry.

The town became a state historic park in 1962, an unlovely place of scattered shacks, vacant hotels, empty saloons, and idle mining equipment. Less living history than leftover history, it lets visitors sense the loneliness and desperation of mining towns in the weathered, rust-brown clapboard on makeshift houses and two leftover horse-drawn hearses. When I visited in mid-May, snow still stood in the streets and muddied the bare spots, and treeless hills stretched to the horizon. I enjoyed the sense of history, and was happy to leave.

By comparison, Owens Valley must have seemed a paradise to white settlers arriving in the 19th century. Streams rushed off the eastern slope of the Sierra and a clear, cold river 50 yards wide lazied along the valley floor and emptied into vast Owens Lake. The water fed grass for cattle, and farmers planted orchards and fields of grain. Then a city took the water away.

Three hundred miles away in Los Angeles, William Mulholland, director of the Department of Water and Power (DWP), saw that his city could not grow without more water. He quietly purchased land in Owens Valley and the rights to the water along with it. With the blessings of President Theodore Roosevelt, who felt that the greater collection of people should be served, Mulholland supervised the building of a 230-mile aqueduct to carry the Owens water to the city. As Los Angeles grew, it bought more and more land, all the time reassuring ranchers that it wanted only surplus water after the valley's needs were met. By 1926 the DWP owned 90 percent of the valley; most of the Sierra runoff was diverted by culverts and gates toward an open cement aqueduct flowing, as it is now, to LA.

Angry locals retaliated. Farmers seized the aqueduct gates and sent the water back into the river. Night riders dynamited holes in the conduit, and Mulholland sent men with tommy guns to guard it in what became known as the Owens Valley Water War. It ended when the ranching and farming economy collapsed in the valley, leaving no constituency to fight for the water.

Litigation continues, however. With no water recharging it, Owens Lake dried into a dust bowl. When the wind blows, which is often, alkaline dust can fill the air for more than 50 miles. One perfectly clear day I drove north on 395 from the south end of the range, confident that at last I would have a view of mighty Mount Whitney unobstructed by rain clouds. From miles away I saw a white plume rising off Owens "Lake," and by the time I reached Lone Pine, Whitney was indistinguishable behind the airborne dust. Valley residents have brought suit against the DWP in an attempt to force mitigation of the dry lakebed with plantings of vegetation.

Aside from the dust, today's heirs to the collapsed economy in other ways count the LA water victory as a curious blessing. Lack of land for development has kept the valley in open rangeland.

"If the DWP hadn't bought up so much property, today there would be a million people living in this valley," I was told by a man fishing for stocked trout in a roadside ditch that ran out of the mountains to join the aqueduct. A real estate agent pointed out that Inyo County is the second largest county in California by acreage, but home to only 18,000 people. Only one and a half percent of the land is privately owned.

One industry in Owens Valley thrived despite the export of water. West of Lone Pine, I walked in canyons between granite buttes and past rounded boulders stacked atop each other like building blocks. The landscape, known as the Alabama Hills, seemed familiar, although I'd never been there before. It was, as folks are fond of saying these days, "just like being in the movies," and well it should be. For years the Alabama Hills were a favorite location for making Hollywood feature films. Dozens of them were Westerns.

This is the Wild West of our cinematic imagination, the granite-spired, sagebrush-studded desert of a thousand posse chases and gunshot ricochets.

A man walks a little taller here in the land of Tom Mix, Gene Autry, Roy Rogers, Hopalong Cassidy, Randolph Scott....

Not only Westerns were filmed in the Alabama Hills, whose name was inspired by the Confederate battleship in the Civil War. This place became the Khyber Pass in *King of the Khyber Rifles*, bush country in *North to Alaska*, Crimea for *The Charge of the Light Brigade*. The biggest production of all was *Gunga Din* (India), with a shoot that lasted ten weeks, employed more than a thousand extras, used hundreds of horses and mules and four elephants, and required construction of a gold-domed Temple of Kali.

"I wore a big, fancy dress in *King of the Khyber Rifles,*" said Dorothy Bonnefin, now a real estate agent in Lone Pine. "Oh it was great fun and paid $35 a day. I also worked at the Dow Hotel, where the stars used to stay: Virginia Mayo, Barbara Stanwyck, Gary Cooper, Tyrone Power...."

Many of the movie horsemen were real cowboys. Leroy Cline grew up on a ranch in the valley and took his first movie job in 1930 at the age of 17. In the following years he appeared in more films than he could list and had a few minor speaking parts.

"Sometimes I'd play a cowboy in the morning and an Indian in the afternoon," said 84-year-old Leroy. "Or they'd dress us in dark clothes and mount us on dark horses and send us galloping across the flats while they panned on us with a camera. Then we'd go back where we started, put on light clothes, get on light-colored horses and gallop across the same flats as the good guys, chasing ourselves! I worked with a lot of the big stars: William Boyd, John Wayne, Cary Grant, Stuart Whitman...."

Although car companies still film commercials here, screen guild requirements killed the steady flow of feature film companies to the arid flats. The industry agreed that anything shot within 300 miles of Hollywood had to employ all professional actors, and Lone Pine is 240 miles away. For cheaper labor, feature film companies moved beyond the limit, but many of the stars return for a film festival each year on Columbus Day weekend.

"One of the town's favorites was Pierce Lyton, who always played the bad guy in Westerns," said Dorothy. "He asked that we boo him when he was introduced." Pierce Lyton? Dorothy dug out a large black and white glossy that resembled a class reunion photo, taken amid the famous boulders. "There he is," she said, and I recognized the menacing eyes and hawkish face of the villain in a dozen movies of my childhood, now smiling pleasantly among aging Hollywood chums Douglas Fairbanks, Jr., Clayton Moore (The Lone Ranger), John Agar, Ann Rutherford....

While moviemakers created scenes in the Alabama Hills, a real-life drama was being played out 110 miles north of Lone Pine. Still needing water as Los Angeles continued to grow, the DWP extended the aqueduct farther up the eastern front to streams feeding Mono Lake.

From a distance, huge Mono Lake, twice the size of San Francisco, looks like welcome relief in an arid basin. A closer view reveals a white alkaline ring around its edge and strange, crusty towers known as tufa rising out of the shallows. Dip your hand into the water, and it feels oily to the touch. Taste it, and it is salty and bitter.

The Sierra runoff that feeds this largest natural lake entirely within California picks up trace amounts of salts and minerals as it flows off the slopes. Undetectable in the streams, they become highly concentrated as the trapped lake water evaporates. Freshwater springs bubbling up through the brine-saturated sands on the bottom raise the crusty towers of tufa, made of calcium carbonate, the principal mineral in limestone. No fish live in waters that are more than twice as salty as the ocean and 80 times more alkaline.

In summer, however, the lake swarms with half-inch-long brine shrimp that feed on microscopic algae. From May through October hordes of gulls, ducks, grebes, and many kinds of shorebirds feed on the shrimp and alkali flies that ring the shore. The latter resemble house flies, but they neither bite nor land on humans. Decades ago, northern Paiutes known as Kutzadika'a collected their pupae and dried them for a protein-rich paste to eat.

In 1941 the DWP began diverting water toward its city from the fresh waters of streams before they reached Mono Lake. By 1981 the lake level had dropped 45 vertical feet. Toxic dust storms blew up from the dry shores, laden with selenium and arsenic.

The lowering lake level concentrated the minerals even more, and populations of both brine shrimp and the alkali flies declined. With the loss of food supply, bird numbers dropped as well. Coyotes walked over a newly raised land bridge to Negit Island to feast on the eggs and chicks of California gulls, which had once nested there in safety. The ecological community of Mono Lake stood in danger of collapse.

In 1976 David Gaines, who had just earned his master's degree in ecology from the University of California at Davis, began a biological study of Mono Lake. His research showed the grim, dusty future that lay ahead, and in 1978 he and some friends formed the Mono Lake Committee. With talks and slide shows, they told the story of the lake's unique ecosystem. "Let the lake speak for itself," Gaines said, and so many listened that lawsuits were filed by the committee and its allies until the DWP was forced to direct water back into the lake. In 1994 the California State Water Resources Control Board limited the amount of water the city can divert from Mono Lake until the lake has been raised 17 feet. Minimum lake levels must be maintained after that.

"The lake is expected to reach the required level sometime around 2015," said Geoffrey McQuilkin, communications director for the Mono Lake Committee, which continues to watchdog the refilling process. "It is rising now. Already the lake has more water than it did four years ago."

Accenting the victory, committee headquarters in the town of Lee

Vining overlooking the lake are in a dance hall built in the 1930s for workers constructing the aqueduct. Los Angeles has made up the difference in the water it lost by improving water conservation and by building reclamation plants that purify waste water enough so it can be used by industry.

Sadly, the hero of Mono Lake never lived to see it saved, although he observed the turning tide of public opinion. Dave Gaines was killed in an automobile accident during a winter storm in 1988.

The water wars lost in earlier years may have driven out many an eastern Sierra resident, but it brought Beryl Rea back to the valley of a thousand pleasant memories.

"As a child, and later as a young married adult, I came to Bishop every summer," she told me as we drove in her truck toward the Owens. "My ancestors were among the first whites to settle the valley, and my grandfather once helped blow up the aqueduct. He also taught me how to cast a fly rod as soon as I was old enough to walk. I fished as a youngster, then taught my boys to love fishing."

Few native trout fight the currents of the swift Sierra streams. Golden trout thrived in the South Fork of the Kern when the first white settlers arrived. They introduced cutthroat trout to the Owens River basin in 1850 by carrying them over Conway Summit in water barrels fastened to freight wagons. Today trout-fishing hopefuls cast their lines in 18,000 miles of California's cooler streams and in 3,581 cold water lakes and reservoirs. The spunky, popular fish accounts for 92,400 jobs in the state.

At loose ends after a midlife divorce, her children grown, Beryl decided to do what she loved in the place that she loved, and moved to Bishop to become a fishing guide. "I've never been so happy in my life," she said.

We pulled up along the lively, clear waters of the upper Owens on a day without a cloud in the sky. Both the White Mountains and Benton Range on one side of the valley and the Sierra on the other glistened with late spring snow. Near the bottom of the Owens, rainbow trout hovered, resting as they moved slowly upstream to spawn. On the way they snack on caddis fly larvae and fork-tailed mayfly nymphs, and cannibalize fish eggs that break loose and tumble downstream. I attempted to imitate a morsel of this buffet by casting upstream and letting my bait drift with the current.

We speak of schools of fish; these were fish that have graduated from the school of sharp hooks. Most have been caught with barbless hooks such as the ones I was using, and released again. They quickly note the difference between loose-drifting nutrients and those attached to a steel shank, and they spit out the latter in a heartbeat.

As my timing improved, the dozen or so half-pounders that I hooked bent my rod in a surging, head-shaking battle for freedom, which I gave them anyway if I managed to bring them to shore. Trout, unlike salmon, swim back downstream after spawning, and live to fight another day.

Stalking the wily trout, a
fly fisherman stands
poised for the tug of a fish
on his line in the Owens
River. Well-schooled
browns and rainbows,
caught and released often,
waste no time rejecting
artificial food. Beyond
looms the eastern rise
of the Sierra, once a
bulwark against early
immigrants, now a
magnificent backdrop for
valley anglers. Some
downstream sections of
the Owens, once dried to
a trickle by aqueduct
diversions to Los Angeles,
have been restored in a
goodwill gesture by the
water company.

"Fish and Game has examined some and found they've been caught and released a dozen or more times, so it doesn't seem to affect them much," said Beryl. Except to make them smarter.

All the ingredients for fly-fishing perfection were present— a clear, cold river flowing between two beautiful mountain ranges; desert, with no trees and few bushes to hang up a line on the back cast; and spunky fish dotting the stream bottom, just waiting to be challenged.

"Days like today, I just love being out here," said Beryl. "I wouldn't care if I never caught a fish." Fat chance of the latter; she reads the water the way a geologist reads rocks, and the fish that dares taste her hand-tied fly is hooked before he can spit.

I claim no bragging rights on the biggest trout I caught, a brown per- haps 27 inches long. Beryl took me to the ranch of Reid Watson, whose love affair with these sporting fish led him to coddle them almost like pets.

"I used to fish these streams with my dad," said Reid, whose gray hair falls to his broad shoulders. "Eventually I came to love raising trout more than catching them."

A successful manufacturer of decorative brass kitchen and bathroom fix- tures, he bought 14 acres and built a series of ponds fed by a stream that runs through the property. As we walked, shaded by plantings of pine and willow, huge trout rose to the surface in anticipation of a meal. Digging into a bucket, Reid sprinkled the surface with vitamin-rich pellets that supplement their natural diet, and the water boiled. "My fish mostly die of old age—about 10 years for an egg-laying female and up to 14 for the males," he said.

He allows catch-and-release fishing by reservation only through Sierra Guide Group. He let me wet a line. On my second cast, one of his monster browns took in my fly, rightfully assuming its daily vitamins had arrived. At the bite of the hook it thrashed in rage, reconfiguring my rod into a perfect U. Then in disdain it turned away, cocked itself at an angle, and calmly resisted my efforts to bring it to shore. The lowered head and slowly wav- ing tail pointed toward me seemed to be sending an obvious message: "Kiss my dorsal." Finally landing it, I admired it briefly, murmured my apologies, and watched it submarine unhurriedly back to the depths, dignity intact.

"This is more than just a hobby," said Reid. "What I learn here about trout I hope will advance the idea of recreating natural streams, getting the fish habitat back to what it was a hundred years ago. Otherwise you're just backing up a truck and dumping fish so campers can haul them in. Might as well open a fish market. I want to see a sustainable harvest, fish spawn- ing naturally, people with two kids coming to catch their limit."

It may be some time before John Wehausen's sheep and lions reach equi- librium, Mono Lake refills itself, and Reid Watson's dream of totally natural streams is realized. In the meantime, lovers of the eastern Sierra are making the best of losing the water wars. ■

FOLLOWING PAGES:
Blowing snow veils Mount Whitney in an air of mystery. The thickest spire at upper right marks the summit, 6 feet short of 14,500 feet. Just ten miles away and two miles lower, the rounded, granite boulders of the Alabama Hills, foreground, mark a true land of fantasy. In dozens of movies made there, the Sierra provided a backdrop that played the Andes, the Himalaya—and itself.

Snow burdens a piñon pine near Mammoth Lakes, a popular ski resort area in the eastern Sierra. A low spot in the range channels moist coastal air to Mammoth, dumping an average of 335 inches of snow on the slopes each year. Mammoth Mountain sits at the edge of 18-mile-wide Long Valley caldera, blasted out 760,000 years ago. The caldera gives evidence of the volcanism that pushed up the Sierra Nevada and still simmers under Earth's crust. A cross-country skier peers into a pool (above) heated by magma below the Earth's surface.

Calling cards of stone rest on the Owens Valley floor, left by Native Americans from 1,000 to 7,000 years ago. Human and animal figures mingle with concentric circles and symbols in a jargon now indecipherable. Desert-dwelling Paiutes probably forced out the unknown ancients a thousand years ago and were in turn displaced by whites in the 19th century. Natives won few battles in the cinematic world of the Alabama Hills (below), scene of many a mock cowboy-and-Indian fight.

FOLLOWING PAGES: Odd-shaped towers of calcium carbonate known as tufa are revealed as the level of Mono Lake drops. Freshwater springs pushing through Mono's carbonated brine and brine-saturated sands create the formations. Brine shrimp in Mono feed hosts of gulls and migratory birds, as do alkali flies on the shores. The gradual lowering of the lake as Los Angeles claimed Mono's tributary streams threatened the ecosystem until lawsuits forced a slow refilling.

Aspens seem to writhe above a carpet of their own fallen leaves in Inyo National Forest. Pressed by heavy snowpack at 8,000 feet while still saplings, the trees retain odd shapes as they con-tinue to grow. Although conifers dominate below tree line in the Sierra Nevada, some 40 species of hardwoods thrive in the range. Today trees cover areas stripped in the 19th century for lumber used in mining and housing.

Storm clouds gather above Owens Valley, but rain rarely reaches the arid lowlands (opposite). The peaks of the eastern escarpment push moist air high to condense before it reaches the desert to the east. Bishop, on the east-ern slope, receives some 5 inches of rain a year, while areas on the western slope get as much as 80 inches. Seeking milder weather, mule deer (above) move onto the valley floor during the Sierra's winters.

A mule-borne honor guard prepares to lead the parade during Mule Days in Bishop, the world's greatest celebration of the cross between a donkey and a horse. Long-faced, long-eared equines from nearly 30 states compete in dressage, cow-cutting, log-skidding, and Roman chariot racing over the Memorial Day weekend. "They're smarter, stronger, and healthier than a horse," says one mule devotee. A beribboned winner looks out from his stall in the show barns (below).

FOLLOWING PAGES:
A full moon casts an eerie glow over Bodie, an abandoned gold-mining town that once boasted a population of 10,000. While the rush lasted, some 30 companies took out 90 to 100 million dollars in gold from tunnels under the town. Now visitors peer through windows to glimpse clues to the town's past: leftover furniture, lessons on a schoolroom blackboard, and a pump organ and wood stove in the Methodist church.

"Don't Fence Me In" led the pop music charts during World War II, but fencing became reality for Japanese-Americans interned at Manzanar in Owens Valley. Viewing them as security risks, the U.S. government moved 10,000 to the former apple orchard near Lone Pine, where many lived more than three years. Some never left, as evidenced by the Manzanar graveyard. "They weren't mistreated," says a former Owens Valley cowboy who trucked food to the camp. "The young people enjoyed themselves." In her book Farewell to Manzanar, *former resident Jeanne Wakatsuki remembers instead diarrhea and blowing dust and calls the camp "a slap in the face you were powerless to challenge."*

EPILOGUE

HOME FROM COLLEGE IN THE 1950S, LAUREL AMES WATCHED DUMP trucks growl to wetlands where the Upper Truckee River empties into Lake Tahoe and drop their loads of dirt. Where the river had once meandered slowly through the reeds, big cranes dug a straight channel so the marsh could be turned into solid ground for more houses.

"I had a vague sense that something wasn't right about all that," Laurel told me, "But in those days, we just didn't know any better."

A lifelong resident of Tahoe, Laurel and others have witnessed the cost of filling in the boggy area, paid in the clarity of the lake's once pristine waters. Scientists now know that wetlands act as filters, trapping silt carried by runoff and keeping lake waters clear. Satellite photos of Tahoe today show dull clouds blossoming into its blue expanse.

"It's hard to describe the crystalline quality the lake used to have," said Laurel. "Being in it was like floating in space, like it wasn't water at all. It makes me heart-sick to go near it now because you don't see water like that any more."

In 1964 a grand development plan for Tahoe called for 18 high-speed freeways and a blizzard of new construction. Architects of the development plan announced proudly that Tahoe would become "...a big city with a hole in the middle." Outraged, and by then aware of the damage being done, Laurel joined the new League to Save Lake Tahoe. Today its 4,500 members send in dues and donations from all 50 states.

"Being an environmentalist in those days was the equivalent of being a Communist," she said. "If you had a league bumper sticker, you risked having your

A cloud invades the blue
waters of Lake Tahoe at
the southern shore devel-
opment called Tahoe Keys.
Landfill to create solid
ground for the houses
destroyed half of the
marsh that filters water
from the Upper Truckee
River entering the lake.

Lawn fertilizers from
homes that line the beach-
front and silt from the dis-
rupted landscape dull the
clarity of waters whose
visibility once exceeded a
hundred feet. Those who
remember the lake as it
once was campaign to
"Keep Tahoe Blue."

windshield broken or your tires slashed. I got nasty phone calls because I was seen as someone who wanted to stop progress."

The league did slow down building activity by helping to instigate an injunction against further development in the 1980s. The result was a plan drawn up in 1987 that prohibits any new subdivisions and limits residential expansion to 300 new houses a year, about one percent of the total number of homes. The plan also limits construction of tourist accommodations.

In 1993 the Sierra Nevada Alliance was formed, pulling together numerous local protection efforts. The League to Save Lake Tahoe became one of its affiliates, and Laurel became the alliance's executive director, expanding her environmental concerns to the entire mountain range. Still, the damage done so far distresses her.

"I'm sad that my hometown is the worst example of tourist development in the Sierra. When I moved here with my parents in 1947, it had 300 people; now there are 45,000. The city is poorly planned, with no architectural scheme, just schlock."

"But you remain here," I pointed out, as we talked at the Sierra Nevada Alliance office in South Lake Tahoe.

"Of course I do," she answered, and gestured toward the view out her window. "Look!"

Thousands of others who live in the splendors of the Sierra Nevada voice distress at the flood of development. Still, they stay, and more keep coming, but perhaps with a new attitude. Laurel senses a change in the way people feel about the Range of Light.

"There's a growing sentiment of feeling responsible for the environment," she said, "a new way of thinking in which people feel they have a role in the future. Our alliance aims at capturing that sense of responsibility and helping people shape the Sierra into a place we can continue to enjoy."

Evidence of that new way of thinking is scattered throughout the range. New directions point to a more sustainable future, and some mistakes of the past will be corrected.

Rochelle Nason, executive director of the League to Save Lake Tahoe, drove me to the wetland that Laurel Ames saw covered in the 1950s. "The California Tahoe Conservancy, a state agency, is going to strip off the covering of fill dirt and recreate the marsh," said Rochelle. "They're even going to fill in the channel and let the stream meander again. The cost may be more than ten million dollars."

Laurel Ames now counts county commissioners among her allies. "They all live in these watersheds and realize that the natural resources make these areas what they are," she said.

"A coalition of 16 counties is trying to build watershed restoration programs. We have 100 years of damage in the Sierra, including poor grazing practices, highways that cut across the watershed, poor timbering techniques, and ski resorts that dump a lot of sediment into streams. We're not against things like ski resorts," she continues. "We just want to see them done right."

Far to the south, fire experts want to see forest fires done right as well. Suppression of fires in the past century has allowed the buildup of dense undergrowth, tinder for massive forest fires in dry years. In past centuries, as research on the giant sequoias has shown, periodic "cool" fires burned off this undergrowth before a massive fuel buildup occurred. Now concerns over air quality squelch even the lighting of controlled, or "prescribed" burns.

"Scientists say we are burning about 10 to 15 percent of what we should be to make a safe forest and to perpetuate the landscape," said William Tweed of Sequoia National Park. "Without adequate controlled burns, eventually a really hot fire can cause great damage and change the nature of the forest."

Woods and water lead the list of concerns in the Sierra Nevada, as residents realize how the two work together. The woods secure the soil so the water doesn't wash it away and hold back the moisture to release it gradually. The water nurtures the woods, provides recreation, and sustains the farms and cities along the coast. Understanding that partnership is a lesson slowly learned over a century and a half.

Early white settlers on the Sierran slopes showed little respect for the land in their search for wealth. Placer miners ripped up streambeds and banks to run gravel through sluice boxes so the heavier gold would settle to the bottom. Silver miners in Nevada denuded forests around Lake Tahoe for timber to shore up tunnels and build houses. Clear-cutting bared slopes to soil erosion well into the 20th century. Hetch Hetchy Valley in today's Yosemite Park was dammed for electrical generation and water storage.

The Sierra Club, founded with the help of John Muir in 1892, two years before the proposal to flood Hetch Hetchy, actively opposed the dam. Though it lost the fight, it gained support for the conservation movement in this country.

The work continues, I was assured by Joe Fontaine, past national president of the Sierra Club and now chairman of its Sierra Nevada Task Force. The task force urges federal officials to better regulate recreational uses of the range, use controlled burns to reduce dangerous fuels, and stop all logging in the southern end of the range. "Many wildlife species depend on old-growth forests for survival," he told me. "Besides, the statistics say the economy in the Sierra Nevada is shifting to tourism anyway, so why spend public money subsidizing the logging industry? We think the money you could save by halting timber sales could be used to restore the forest."

For all the Sierra Club's history of battling for its namesake, Fontaine says he dislikes doomsday prophecies about the range. "It's still a spectacularly beautiful place," he said. "We want people to know about that beauty so they know that it's worth saving."

The worst damage in the Sierra came from creating canyons, not filling them up. In the late 19th century, hydraulic mining knocked down hills and washed them away with the invention of the water cannon. The process was based on the same principle at work when you put your thumb over the end of a garden hose to project a smaller but more powerful spray. A water cannon channeled water through a hose from a higher elevation to a lower one, allowing it to exit through a much smaller hole. Powered by the weight of water behind it, the high-speed jet of liquid obliterated whole hillsides so miners could get at the gold underground.

By the mid-1850s, all the easy placer gold in the streams had been picked over, and the independent gold prospector had little chance of striking it rich. But streambeds change through the millennia, and miners knew that gold washed down earlier might be in an ancient bed high and dry on a hillside. With water cannons,

Carved in the quest for gold, a clay spire rises at Malakoff Diggins State Historic Park. In the world's largest hydraulic gold mine, 19th century miners hosed away entire hillsides, directing loosened soil and gravel through sluices to capture gold fragments. The technique stripped organic matter from the land, which is still recovering a century later. Downstream the silt ruined farmland and caused rivers to flood towns, resulting in landmark legislation that prohibits the dumping of tailings into rivers and streams.

mining companies could dissolve the hillsides and direct their silt load through sluice boxes to trap the heavy gold.

The largest hydraulic gold mining operation in the world unfolded at the Malakoff ravine north of Nevada City. In 1866 a single miner bought out his partners and rounded up six investors in San Francisco to form the North Bloomfield Gravel Mining Company. Using water from dammed-up streams, the company ran 100,000 tons of gravel through the sluice boxes every day when operating at top capacity in 1876. When working at full capacity day and night, the operation produced more than $100,000 a month in gold, and was expected to continue for 30 to 40 years.

Gold fragments settled in the sluices, but the silt continued downstream into the South Yuba River, on to the Sacramento, and all the way to the sea. San Francisco Bay ran brown. Silt filled up rivers, causing them to flood and inundate farms in the Central Valley. Towns built levees to contain the waters, but the silt continued to build up until the bottom of the Yuba, flowing by Marysville, was higher than the town. Inevitably, the levees gave way in one ferocious flood, causing loss of life and extensive property damage and leaving three feet of mud in Marysville streets.

Outraged property owners filed a petition with the state legislature. Years of skirmishing in the courts followed, and in 1884 Judge Lorenzo Sawyer issued a permanent injunction against hydraulic mining. His decision may have marked the first time in this country that environmental considerations overrode a major lucrative commercial operation.

More than a century later, walking a trail through the Malakoff Diggins State Historic Park, I was a wanderer in a ruined land. Orange gashes lined the banks of what was once a ravine and is now a broad valley holding shallow, fetid water. Vegetation struggles to grow, for the hoses pummeled any light organic matter and sent it downstream, leaving rock and clay. Perhaps it's the nature of parks, but somehow the operation is still glorified.

"The great Malakoff mine pit with its colorful cliffs," reads a park brochure, "is 7,000 feet long, as much as 3,000 feet wide, and nearly 600 feet deep in places."

FOLLOWING PAGES:
Rainbow over a clearcut
hillside in Stanislaus
National Forest signals a
pot of gold in sales for the
timber industry and a
damaged watershed to

environmentalists. A
study of the Sierra
requested by Congress
states that logging roads
and lost tree cover con-
tribute to the degradation
of the Sierra's streams.

In a 1973 film shown at park headquarters, an enthusiastic narrator said that the mining operation "...was a tribute to the argonauts who set nature against itself, using the rivers to tear down the mountains." Hydraulic mining, the narrator added with a touch of regret, "...did not die because it was inefficient; it died because it served so few and injured so many."

The Malakoff Diggins represents a very small part of the Sierra Nevada. Forests, on the other hand, cover perhaps three-quarters of the entire range; over the past century and a half they have changed radically. A majority of the oldest and largest trees have been cut down, and the secondary woods that replaced them have become dense and brushy—fuel for the much-feared wildfires. Increasingly, people are moving into these altered woodlands, putting themselves and their property at risk.

By studying the numbers of old-growth trees that remain in our national parks, exempt from logging, researchers have determined that less than a quarter of the ancient forests that once existed in the range now remain. Two-thirds of the old-growth trees are in national forests, and one-third in national parks. Except in places that are difficult to reach, those on private lands have been felled for lumber. Likewise in national forests, logging roads and permits have made the big trees accessible for harvest, although temporary guidelines now prohibit cutting any trees more than 30 inches in diameter.

The question of how many trees of any size should be taken from the Sierra remains a contested issue. Rose Comstock, past president CONTINUED ON PAGE 188

PRECEDING PAGES:
Bumper crop of bunga-lows sprouts in the foothills east of Sacra-mento after an Intel plant located outside the city. A shift by industries from high-rent municipal areas to low-ticket rural loca-tions feeds both urban sprawl and downtown decay. A coalition of busi-nesses now encourages cul-tural and commercial growth in core areas to spur the building of new houses in old neighbor-hoods. The result: pleasant towns for living and open countryside for recreation.

In the New West, skies may be cloudy all day and night. Visitors to Moro Rock in Sequoia National Park sometimes view the scenery darkly (above), through air pollution drifting from distant Los Angeles. Wood stoves and fireplaces lend warmth and cheer but also leave a blanket of evening smoke over towns like Truckee, north of Lake Tahoe (right). Restrictions on wood burning may be needed to clear the night air, and tightening the controls on auto emissions could someday help clean the skies over parks in the Sierra Nevada.

Rivers of headlights and oceans of neon emblazon the night at South Lake Tahoe along Route 50. Casinos and commercial strips hug the shores of the lake that Samuel Clemens described in 1861 as "surely...the fairest picture the whole earth affords." A sleepy town of 300 half a century ago, South Lake Tahoe has burgeoned into a city approaching 50,000 with thousands more in resorts and residences around the shore. Millions of vacationers come for year-round activities that include skiing, gambling, hiking, floor shows, and golf. Legislators of both Nevada and California have created a regional planning agency to help control growth. Non-profit groups pushing for reforms report increased cooperation between developers and environmentalists.

CONTINUED FROM PAGE 179 of the California branch of Women in Timber, believes in prudent logging as a way of saving logging jobs and preventing disastrous fires. "We're concerned citizens who want to maintain the wise use of a resource that sustains our rural economies and meets consumers' high demand for wood fiber," she told me. "By not removing dead trees we're left with an average of 56 snags per acre in the Sierra—fuel for wildfires."

Scott Hoffman Black of the Sierra Nevada Forest Protection Campaign maintains that too many trees have already been cut, endangering certain species and altering forest systems that are not easily replaced. The spotted owl has occupied center stage in the old-growth timber controversy, he says, but other creatures also depend on ancient forests for survival. They include the Sierra Nevada red fox, the pileated woodpecker, the northern flying squirrel, the marten, and the fisher.

For humans, the greatest immediate damage from too much logging may be the change in that most precious Sierra resource, water. In a landmark scientific study known as the Sierra Nevada Ecosystem Project (SNEP), requested by Congress and submitted in June 1996, researchers determined that "aquatic-riparian systems are the most altered and impaired habitats of the Sierra (Nevada)." SNEP listed excessive sediments in the water as one of the major problems. Logging, and the 18,000 miles of logging roads in the range, it noted, are among the chief culprits.

John Lundquist sees both sides of the logging question. He started cutting trees for lumber companies in 1975 at the age of 21 and continued until a back injury forced him to quit in 1997.

"I looked forward to work every day," he told me in the mobile home where he lives with his wife and two daughters on the shores of Lake Almanor in the heavily forested north. "I loved the challenge of felling the trees where you want them, and I loved being in the woods. I loved it all, except..." he added, as more realistic memories intruded, "...walking uphill to my next tree while carrying all my equipment, with sweat running down my face and my muscles burning."

"At the same time, I felt we were doing some things wrong, like clear-cutting on steep slopes. I was unpopular with environmentalists because I cut down trees, and I was unpopular with a lot of loggers because they considered me a greenie. For a long time I think the pendulum had swung too far on the side of lumber production, but now maybe it's too far the other way. The Forest Service's job, after all, is to maintain a balance."

John returned to school for a two-year program that will allow him to continue to work in the woods as a forestry technician. In the meantime he hopes to build a home to join the hundreds of others now ringing Lake Almanor.

The attraction of the woodlands has changed economies throughout the Sierra. The SNEP study showed that compared to a quarter century ago, employment in the timber industry now generates far less income than commuters who work elsewhere, retirees who receive benefits, and visitors who come to have fun. The tree harvest from federal forests in California was cut in half between 1992 and 1998.

Reflecting a general change in federal attitude, the chief of the U.S. Forest Service, Mike Dombeck, said in a message to his staff in mid-1998: "We need to do a better job talking about, and managing for, the values that are so important to so many people. Values such as wilderness and roadless areas, clean water, conservation of species, old-growth forests' naturalness—these are the reasons most Americans cherish their public lands." In July 1998 the Forest Service launched studies that may lead to new management of the Sierra forests, both public—and through collaboration with other landowners—private.

"Society is telling us that it wants to see more emphasis on fish and wildlife and recreation in the national forests, and less timber cutting," said Matt Mathes, Forest Service spokesman in the regional office in San Francisco. "Already there has been a definite shift from cutting old growth to cutting smaller trees, as a means of thinning out the density that can lead to wildfires.

"By noting the results of the SNEP report and hearing comments from the public, we're working toward a long-term framework for good management of all forests in the Sierra, no matter who the owners might be."

What is a sustainable use of Sierra Nevada forests? The question lingers in the face of continued forest harvest and residential development, and sometimes brings together factions that have long been at odds. In a few cases, planning for public forest use is being done in cooperation with local people, including poet Gary Snyder.

The road from avant-garde poet to environmental visionary has included some interesting stops for the Pulitzer Prize-winning writer. In the 1950s he spent time with novelist Jack Kerouac, did readings with beat generation poet Allen Ginsberg, and in 1967 participated in the "First Great Human Be-In" in San Francisco's Golden Gate Park. During the 1960s he studied Zen Buddhism in a monastery in Japan.

But Gary the writer and philosopher has also been a trail worker for the National Park Service, a fire lookout, and a logger. Today his attitudes about the use of Sierra forests grow out of those experiences, out of a lifetime of contemplation and study, and out of living in the forest itself.

"Back in the fifties we'd jump in a car on a weekend and head for the high country," he told me. "The Sierra was remote, and those of us who could spend time in it were really lucky. We didn't think much about the lower elevations. Now people are moving into those areas; they are well-educated people who know a lot about ecology and care about issues such as biodiversity."

Gary Snyder among them. On a hill north of Nevada City, we talked in a weathered barn that had been converted into his writing studio, books carefully shelved from floor to rafters and pines looming outside. Snyder justifies his presence by remaining a "low-impact" resident on the 100 acres he owns. Two mule deer browsed nearby as I drove up, and Snyder said he once saw a cougar sitting right outside a window where his stepdaughter Mika practiced piano.

Gary generates his own electricity from solar panels and demands no network of water systems, sewers, or paved roads to the log and frame structures where he lives with his wife, writer Carole Koda, and Mika. "The problem," said Gary, "is that people want to move into the woods but live like they did in the city."

Those who would label him a radical might be surprised to learn that he favors cutting some trees, but in a new and different way. To study how forests should be handled, Gary and several neighbors who live on San Juan Ridge above the Yuba River have formed the Yuba Watershed Institute (YWI). In 1991 the Institute signed an agreement with the Bureau of Land Management to be partners in planning the management of 1,250 acres of forestland in the watershed. Later the Forest Service asked YWI to submit a plan for another 2,400 acres of national forest nearby.

"So far, we've been studying relationships in the forest and discussing possibilities for change, such as retooling sawmills so they can handle smaller logs. And we're getting other local people involved by conducting educational programs in the community. Residents should be part of the decision-making process because they know their area better than anyone else."

He drove me through woods near his home that have been thinned by a brush-shredding machine, a possible alternative to controlled burns. "We're not talking about short-term logging practices; it should be possible to have a 500-year logging plan that would provide both jobs and biodiversity, although perhaps not at the level of profit that industrial timber companies expect."

The prospect of local people helping plan for the use of federal lands makes many in the government uncomfortable, admits Deane Swickard, area manager for the BLM, who set up the partnership with the YWI.

"In the past, the government has come up with ideas about how the land should be managed, and the public has opposed them. It seemed to me there must be a better way. We can't be a green gestapo lording it over the locals. The people in the YWI are very accomplished, and willing helpers, so why shouldn't they be involved? I'm working with two other groups in a similar arrangement."

The more we learn about the way the world works, the better we can see the steps required to keep it working. How serious are we about taking them?

"I'm sure the lure of money will not abate," said Laurel Ames of Sierra Nevada Alliance, "but there's potential for much better stewardship of the land."

Even many moneymakers now recognize the advantages of saving the Sierra.

The shorn base of a giant sequoia provides a picnic site for visitors to Kings Canyon National Park. A century earlier, sawyers toppled the giant trees for use as lumber. As protection came for the sequoias, say optimists, so may it come on a larger scale to all the Sierra Nevada. Those who fight to save the natural quality of the mountains say they detect a greater awareness of the damage caused by human activity and a mounting determination to avoid repeating the mistakes of the past.

FOLLOWING PAGES:
A new day in the Sierra finds a winter camper in Eldorado National Forest preparing breakfast by the glow of lantern and headlamp. Ahead stretch hours in the solitude of wilderness and the silence of the woods, which have long drawn fugitives from crowded cities. Preservationists also hope for a new day in the Sierra, when planned development and careful use of a priceless natural resource can offer visitors a chance to follow John Muir's advice: "Climb the mountains and get their good tidings."

Nearly 500 enterprises ranging in size from the Bank of America to small restaurants and motels have joined the Sierra Business Council (SBC), a five-year-old organization based on the premise that losing the environment means losing business.

"We expect the regional population to double by 2020," said associate director Tracy Grubbs at SBC headquarters in Truckee. "We want our economy to continue to thrive through that increase. We advocate, for example, honoring the compact town design of our past and maintaining a clean break between town and country. In the long run, everyone is better off, including business people and residents."

For thousands of years the region maintained a balance, with little impact from the Native Americans who lived on its slopes and ventured occasionally into its highlands. Now it seems, the more sophisticated we become, the more difficult it is to let nature run its course. Attempts to do so, fortunately, appear to be under way.

At the Indian Cultural Museum in Yosemite National Park I asked Julia Parker, practitioner of the ancient skills of the Yosemite Miwok and Paiute, what the new custodians of the Sierra could learn from the Native Americans. "Respect for the land and how it is used," she answered without hesitation.

The last totally primitive Native American encountered in California, perhaps in the whole United States, is believed to have been a man named Ishi. The only survivor of an isolated group of Yahi, he was captured and regarded as a "wild man" when he came out of the hills in a desperate search for food in 1911.

Befriended by anthropologist Alfred Kroeber, Ishi learned some English and became a bridge between the primitive and modern worlds before he died of tuberculosis in 1913. His attitudes toward white civilization serve as a reminder that technological arrogance is not the best answer for the Sierra Nevada.

"He looked upon us as sophisticated children—smart but not wise," remembered Saxton Pope, a physician and an admirer of Ishi. "We knew many things, and much that is false. He knew nature, which is always true."

Perhaps a new search for truth will bring a brighter future to the Range of Light. ■

INDEX

ADDITIONAL READING

Readers may wish to consult the *National Geographic
Index* for related articles and books including:

Kenneth Brower, *Yosemite: An American Treasure*

William R. Gray, *The Pacific Crest Trail*

Tom Melham, *John Muir's Wild America*

*National Geographic's Guide to the National Parks
of the United States*

*National Parks of North America: Canada,
United States, Mexico.*

The following titles may also be of interest:

Austin, Mary, *The Land of Little Rain*

Elna Bakker, *An Island Called California*

Craig D. Bates, *The Miwok in Yosemite*

Ezra Bowen, *The High Sierra; The Complete Gold Country Guide Book*

Richard Dillon, *Fool's Gold: The Decline and Fall of
Captain John Sutter of California*

Lary Dilsaver and William Tweed, *Challenge of the
Big Trees: A Resource History of Sequoia and Kings
Canyon National Parks*

Don C. Erman, editor, *Status of the Sierra Nevada:
The Sierra Nevada Ecosystem Project* (CD-ROM)

Francis P. Farquhar, *History of the Sierra Nevada*

David Gaines, *Mono Lake Guidebook*

Dwight Holing, *The Smithsonian Guides to Natural
America: The Far West—California and Nevada*

Dave Holland, *On Location in Lone Pine: A Pictorial
Guide to Movies Shot in and Around California's
Alabama Hills*

J.S. Holliday, *The World Rushed In: The California Gold
Rush Experience*

Sue Irwin, *California's Eastern Sierra: A Visitor's Guide*

Verna R. Johnston, *Sierra Nevada: The Naturalist's
Companion*

Holway R. Jones, *John Muir and the Sierra Club:
The Battle for Yosemite*

Liza Ketchum, *The Gold Rush*

Muir, John, *My First Summer in the Sierra*

Gerald W. Olmsted, *The Best of the Sierra Nevada*

Tim Palmer, *The Sierra Nevada: A Mountain Journey*

William E. Riebsame, editor, *Atlas of the New West*

Marc Reisner, *Cadillac Desert: The American West and
Its Disappearing Water*

R. J. Secor, *The High Sierra: Peaks, Passes, and Trails*

National Park Service, *Sequoia and Kings Canyon:
A Guide to Sequoia and Kings Canyon National Parks*

Genny Smith, editor, *Deepest Valley*

Steve Sorensen, *Day Hiking Kings Canyon*

Douglas H. Strong, *Tahoe: An Environmental History*

Time-Life Books, *The Forty-Niners*

Mark Twain, *Roughing It*

Paul Webster, *The Mighty Sierra: Portrait of a
Mountain World*

Stephen Whitney, *A Sierra Club Naturalist's Guide to
the Sierra Nevada*

John Wilcock, editor, *Northern California*

Wilderness Society, *The Federal Forest Lands of the
Sierra Nevada: Citizens' Guide to the Sierra Nevada
Ecosystem Project (SNEP) Report*

Thomas Winnett, *Mt. Whitney*

George Wuerthner, *California's Sierra Nevada*

NOTES ON CONTRIBUTORS

Born in the Midwest, freelance photographer PHIL
SCHERMEISTER began his career as a newspaper photographer. Over the past 12 years, assignments for the
National Geographic Society have taken him to Mexico's
Copper Canyon, Banff National Park in Canada, and
numerous locations in the United States. During his cov-
erage for this book, he hiked, backpacked, skied, and
paddled throughout the Sierra Nevada over a period of
six months. Phil and his wife, Laureen, live in the Sierra
Nevada foothills town of Sonora, California.

National Geographic staff writer for 25 years, NOEL
GROVE contributed 28 bylined articles for NATIONAL
GEOGRAPHIC magazine and chapters for five National
Geographic books. He is the author of *Wild Lands for
Wildlife: America's National Refuges,* published by
National Geographic. He also wrote *Preserving Eden* and
Birds of North America. Assignments have taken the
author to all 50 states in the U.S. and to more than 60
other countries. Noel free lances from his home near
Middleburg, Virginia, and is editor of *SEJournal,* a
quarterly publication for environmental writers.

ACKNOWLEDGMENTS

The Book Division wishes to thank the many individuals, groups, and organizations mentioned or quoted in
this publication for their help and guidance.
   In addition we are grateful to Christine Cowles,
Carolyn Fregulia, Katherine Haines, John Hutchinson,
Ralph Moore, Sara Pence, Diana Pietrasanta, Sue Russell, Sally Taylor, Ty Wivell, and Harvey Young. Also,
we thank editors Martha Christian and Lyn Clement
for their reviews of the final text.

Range of Light: The Sierra Nevada

Photographs by Phil Schermeister
Text by Noel Grove

Published by the National Geographic Society

John M. Fahey, Jr. *President and Chief Executive Officer*
Gilbert M. Grosvenor *Chairman of the Board*
Nina D. Hoffman *Senior Vice President*

Prepared by the Book Division

William R. Gray *Vice President and Director*
Charles Kogod *Assistant Director*
Barbara A. Payne *Editorial Director and Managing Editor*
David Griffin *Design Director*

Staff for this Book

Charles Kogod *Project Editor*
Rebecca Beall Barns *Text Editor*
David Griffin *Art Director*
Tom Powell *Illustrations Editor*
Anne E. Withers *Researcher*
Carl Mehler *Director of Maps*
Thomas L. Gray *Map Researcher*
Michelle H. Picard *Map Production*
R. Gary Colbert *Production Director*
Lewis R. Bassford *Production Project Manager*
Richard Wain *Production Manager*
Meredith C. Wilcox *Illustrations Assistant*
Peggy J. Candore *Assistant to the Director*
Kevin G. Craig *Staff Assistants*
Dale-Marie Herring
Anne Marie Houppert *Indexer*

Manufacturing and Quality Management

George V. White *Director*
John T. Dunn *Associate Director*
Vincent P. Ryan *Managers*
Gregory Storer
James J. Sorensen *Budget Analyst*

The world's largest nonprofit scientific and educational organization, the National Geographic Society was founded in 1888 "for the increase and diffusion of geographic knowledge." Since then it has supported scientific exploration and spread information to its more than nine million members worldwide.

The National Geographic Society educates and inspires millions every day through magazines, books, television programs, videos, maps and atlases, research grants, the National Geography Bee, teacher workshops, and innovative classroom materials.

The Society is supported through membership dues and income from the sale of its educational products. Members receive NATIONAL GEOGRAPHIC magazine—the Society's official journal—discounts on Society products, and other benefits.

For more information about the National Geographic Society and its educational programs and publications, please call 1-800-NGS-LINE (647-5463), or write to the following address:

National Geographic Society
1145 17th Street N.W.
Washington, D.C. 20036-4688
U.S.A.

Visit the Society's Web site at
www.nationalgeographic.com.

Library of Congress CIP Data:

Grove, Noel.
    Range of light : the Sierra Nevada / by Noel Grove ; photographed by Phil Schermeister.
        p.   cm.
    Includes index.
    ISBN 0-7922-7840-2
    ISBN 0-7922-7841-0
    1. Sierra Nevada (Calif. and Nev.)—Description and travel. 2. Sierra Nevada (Calif. and Nev.)—Pictorial works. 3. Natural history—Sierra Nevada (Calif. and Nev.) I. Schermeister, Phil. II. Title.
    F868.S5 G76 1999
    979.4'4—dc21   99-11783
                                                  CIP

WITHDRAWN